50 *Really*
Exot█████████s

A Fur-and-Feather-Free Guide to the Most Lovable Tarantulas, Tortoises, Snakes, Frogs, Lizards, and Other Creatures

David Manning

Collins

An Important Note on Owning Exotic Pets

This book discusses a number of animal species as pets. It is essential to note that pet ownership laws vary from state to state and even from city to city. Do not assume that a pet is legal because it is mentioned in this book or available in a pet store. Before purchasing any exotic pet, find out if the species is legal and/or requires a special permit or license. You should first contact your local government (such as your city hall or county office) to ask if there are any relevant laws. It is also a good idea to check with your local health department, which often has jurisdiction in this area. You should then contact your state Department of Agriculture. Keep checking until you have received an authoritative response that there are no laws prohibiting pet ownership of a particular species and also that the species is not protected as native wildlife in your state. The author and the publisher are not responsible for the failure to check the legality of any pet you are considering.

www.collins.co.uk

Collins is a registered trademark of HarperCollins Publishers Limited

Text © David Manning

ISBN: 978-0-06-149181-8
FIRST U.S. EDITION published 2008

HarperCollins books may be purchased for educational, business, or sales promotional use. For information in the United States, please write to: Special Markets Department, HarperCollins Publishers, 10 East 53rd Street, New York, NY 10022.

11 10 09 08
6 5 4 3 2 1

Created by: **SP Creative Design**
Editor: **Heather Thomas**
Designer: **Rolando Ugolini**
Series design: **Mark Thomson**

Photography
All images by Simon Murrell and David Manning, www.animalark.com.au
except for the following:
Jed Currey: Woma Python and Black Headed Python
Exo Terra vivariums Hagen
Can O' Food Zoo Med
Chris Mattison: American Green Toad

Printed and bound by **Printing Express Ltd., Hong Kong**

Contents

Introduction

By picking up this book, you are probably either considering keeping exotic pets, or you already have an interest in them. Not only are many of these creatures extremely beautiful to look at but they are also much simpler to look after than some of the more traditional pet mammals and birds with whom we choose to share our lives.

Among the most popular pet amphibians, tree frogs are remarkably easy to look after and many species are suitable for handling by keepers.

Which species?

While many species of exotic pets are easy to care for, there are some obvious considerations to bear in mind before purchasing one of these pets. In the case of children, for example, a parent or another adult must ultimately be responsible for the welfare of the chosen species. As a responsible herpetologist, in this book I have concentrated on species that meet the following criteria.

They are suitable for the novice keeper

I have tried to promote the care of the most easy-to-keep and interesting species that are not too demanding in terms of time or space. However, at the same time, I have also included some of the most popular animals, such as chameleons and iguanas.

They are available from pet stores or breeders

All the species featured in the book are widely available from specialty breeders or pet stores and, wherever possible, from captive-bred stock. This will ensure that they are free from internal and external parasites and are most likely to adapt successfully to new homes.

Ease of care

I have listed the species that are featured within each section of this book in an "ease-of-care" order. The easiest to keep appear first, graduating to those species that are more demanding in terms of equipment, space, owner's time, and maintenance.

Conservation

Loss of natural habitat for housing or agricultural development, along with pollution and other negative human actions, is having a colossal impact on the rapidly decreasing numbers of reptiles, amphibians, and invertebrates globally. An estimated 1,856 species of amphibians, about 32 percent of known species,

Many snakes, such as this Royal Python, are easy to keep and breed as pets.

Opposite: The endearing Leopard Gecko is a small lizard that is easy to tame and can be kept in small groups together in the vivarium.

are "globally threatened" according to International Union for the Conservation of Nature (IUCN).

Captive breeding

For many creatures, captive breeding offers an opportunity for their continued survival. It is hoped that one day these can be reintroduced into the wild if their habitats can be saved. Captive breeding also helps reduce pressure on wild populations, teaches us about their life cycle and husbandry, and provides us with healthier livestock. It is remarkably satisfying when you watch a snake hatch from an egg, or a batch of tadpoles metamorphose into their adult form.

These Australian Green Tree Frogs are a popular choice of pet and are widely available from captive bred stocks in the United States, Europe, and Australia.

Responsible ownership and husbandry

The collection of certain animals from the wild and their trade between countries may be—rightly or wrongly—illegal. However, it is important that wherever you happen to live, you adhere to both your local and national rules and regulations. Responsible pet ownership and husbandry are always the right way to proceed.

A rewarding pastime

This book will help you not only to select a pet that suits you and your circumstances but also to learn more about these fascinating exotic animals and the whole subject of herptoculture, which can become a vastly rewarding and absorbing pastime for many keepers. A comprehensive range of the most popular species available are examined, with enough detail for even a novice keeper to successfully care for these intriguing creatures.

1   The vivarium

People have been keeping more unusual
pets for centuries, and many are surprisingly
interesting and easy-to-keep companions.
With patience and careful husbandry, it is
possible, if desired, for the pet keeper to both
enjoy and breed some of these wonderful
creatures. In the home, a vivarium can be a
beautiful and enchanting miniature habitat
that you and your pet can enjoy.

Choosing your pet

Before purchase check with your local or state governments to see if there are any restrictions on exotic pet species in your area. Pet ownership laws vary from state to state and sometimes even from city to city, so a creature mentioned in this book or even for sale in a pet store may not be legal to own.

must know

Ask the person who is supplying the animal plenty of questions. If they are reputable, they will expect you to ask them questions and should be able to assist you in selecting a suitable individual.

First steps

Read all about the animals and their care and then decide on a species that will suit you and your circumstances best. Consider the accommodation, equipment, feeding, and handling requirements.

Don't rush

Taking time is important—just like setting up an aquarium for fish, you need to check that a vivarium is running smoothly and the equipment functioning correctly before buying your pet. Monitor the temperature gradient and the humidity to ensure you have created the right environment.

With an aquarium or semiaquatic setup, it is essential that you allow the water to age/mature, ideally for seven to ten days, so that the system functions to optimum effect.

Selection

Now that the vivarium is set up properly, you are ready to select your pet. To increase the chances of keeping your pet healthy and in tip-top condition you will need to choose a healthy individual, preferably a juvenile that has been captive bred by an established breeder.

Always look for specimens that:
- are bright-eyed and alert looking
- are good feeders
- do not bolt, flee, or cower.

Avoid specimens that:
- have a dirty vent (the external opening of the urinary and genital systems)—caked-on fecal matter is a sure sign of illness
- cannot support their weight or walk in an uncomfortable manner
- have crooked limbs and lumps that are not a feature of that species
- have little fat reserves on the tail
- are the runt of a litter/batch.

Rearing containers

It is probable that many of the baby animals that are purchased have been reared in what at first may seem like unsuitable conditions—plastic boxes, 10 x 4 x 6 inches (25 x 10 x 15 cm.) with tiny air holes drilled into the lid for ventilation. Each box, containing a baby snake, for example, will be lined with paper and equipped with a tiny shelter and water dish. Providing it is warmed with a heater pad or cable, this is the ideal rearing container in which to nurture a young snake and raise it as a tame pet. To suddenly put such a fragile animal into your new larger vivarium can be a shock. It may feel vulnerable and refuse to feed or it may hide, never to be seen again. It is best to leave the young snake in its rearing container, and when you feel the time is right—once it has grown a bit and feeds regularly— transfer it into its larger permanent setup.

Take time to select a healthy individual animal. This Spadefoot Toad is in excellent condition. It looks well fed and is alert and bright-eyed.

must know

Do not handle animals after they have eaten or when they are about to molt or slough. If you are transporting a pet, it must be comfortable and at a temperature and humidity level that will not cause suffering.

Where to obtain stock

Joining a reptile club or herpetological society is an excellent way to obtain stock, find breeders, and get up-to-date information on suitable species. Ask your family or friends; you will be surprised how someone always seems to know someone who has an interest in these pets. The Internet is a good source for information, with thousands of web sites devoted to reptiles, amphibians, and invertebrates. The various reptile magazines published in most countries are full of advertisements, and your local library will have other books on the subject. Even if your local pet store does not stock reptiles, they will probably know where to start looking.

Scientific or Latin names

People can easily get confused if only the common names are used to discuss particular species. In the United States, the small African Python is called the Ball Python, but in Great Britain it is known as the

Regular handling will enable both you and your pet to get to know each other better.

Royal Python. To avoid any confusion, zoologists use Latin names to describe all animals and plants. Karl von Linne, or Linnaeus as he is normally referred to, developed this two-name, or binomial, system in the 1700s. It is a useful tool, helping us classify and understand the natural world with a universally recognized system. So from China to the United States, the small African Python is known as *Python regius* and no one mistakes it for any other snake.

The Latin name is written in italics and usually follows the common name. In scientific journals, the common names are usually not used. When purchasing a pet, learn the Latin name and use it to avoid any confusion when doing further research.

Children, as well as adults, enjoy regular interaction with tame and friendly species of reptile.

Handling pets

Many of the species featured in this book are among the most handleable of all herptiles, and people can get great pleasure from this close contact with nature. However, some species are enjoyed aesthetically, and, once in the vivarium, they are handled only when they are removed for cleaning to take place.

When handling your pet, check the environment is safe—for example, do you need to close a door or window to prevent it from escaping if it takes flight or tries to hop away. Minimize the danger of a fall by sitting at a table or on the floor. Your pet is not a toy and handling by children must always be closely supervised by an adult.

Juvenile animals should only be handled occasionally and for short periods until they become tame or conditioned enough to sit still. Feeding your pet after a handling session is a good way to condition it to accepting human contact as a positive stimulus.

Adult supervision is always highly recommended when children handle small and delicate pets.

Amphibians

The mucus-covered skin of many amphibians protects them from bacterial infections and makes them difficult to handle. It is best to handle them with wet hands. Some amphibians have toxins in their skin, so be careful if you have any open wounds, because handling them may let toxins enter your body. Do not be worried about handling them; during educational talks, my own tree frogs have been handled by many people several days a week for several years with no ill effect to man or frog. Most amphibians can be held in cupped hands or scooped up into small containers for transportation. These can be filled with a damp sponge to provide moisture. However, you must transport totally aquatic species in water.

Lizards

Supported by caring hands, this gecko is learning to tolerate being handled by its keeper.

The dry skin and docility of the lizards that are featured in this book make them ideal candidates for more intimate contact—they are among the most handleable species. However, lizards should never be lifted by the tail—their ability to "drop" them is well known.

Snakes

Small snakes are easily supported in the hand—most will wrap around your fingers or wrist to feel comfortable. Never dangle them from the neck or tail, but support them along the length of their body. Hold heavier species firmly and support their weight. The novice keeper should not handle untamed snakes, because they need proper restraining. Transport your snakes in cloth bags or tied pillowcases. Smaller species or juveniles may be transported in their plastic rearing boxes.

Invertebrates

Many invertebrates are delicate and need careful handling. Do not disturb them if they are molting. Caution is advised at all times when handling these creatures because most species have tiny hooklike claws that can easily get tangled up with clothing or may even snag a small child's skin. If in doubt, do not handle them.

must know

The benefits of keeping a vivarium pet can be summarized as follows:
1 You are unlikely to be allergic to an animal that has no fur or feathers.
2 Reptiles, amphibians, and invertebrates may be kept in locations that prohibit the care of other species—for example, an apartment with no yard.
3 They are generally silent and do not require regular walks, annual veterinary inoculations, or grooming.
4 Most species are easily maintained, requiring at most only a 10-minute daily feed and a cleaning regime that takes an hour or so each week.
5 Most species are content to live in a vivarium. Some, such as Milk Snakes, prefer small, secure accommodation—larger units may cause them stress.
6 Although a relationship may be established, vivarium pets, unlike dogs, will not be emotionally dependent on you. They will not feel lonely if you are out of the house during the day and many can be left safely for a weekend.
7 These fascinating creatures can help nurture an interest in natural history, conservation, and, hopefully, a respect for all living things.

Housing your pet

To create the right environment for your pet, you must have an understanding of the types of accommodation and equipment that are available. Making the right choice is essential and should ensure that your pet enjoys a long and healthy life.

must know

Always buy the best-quality accommodation and equipment you can afford. Don't try to save money on what may be the most important aspect of your pet's welfare. The housing and equipment can cost more than the pet itself, but it will last and also provide an environment that is beneficial to the long-term well-being and health of your pet.

The vivarium

A vivarium or aquarium can be a beautiful and enchanting miniature habitat, which both you and your pet can enjoy. Many purpose-built vivaria are available, making it easy for you to select a secure unit and create the ideal conditions for the animals in your care. I generally encourage larger vivaria for most pets—they let you keep more individuals together and even to establish a community setup. The range of suitable vivaria can be divided into three main categories.

Glass

The most versatile option for housing is glass. You can keep any animal mentioned in this book in a glass vivarium or aquarium. The latest Exo Terra vivariums (as pictured) are excellent and have a simple locking mechanism to prevent any escapes; they are also well ventilated. I currently keep snakes, lizards, frogs, and praying mantids in different-size ones. Their disadvantage is they can't be stacked one on top of the other once your collection expands. Glass is easy to clean, hygienic, and gives all-round visibility. However, it is important to provide adequate cover and hiding places, so that your pet does not feel exposed.

Wood

Wooden or particleboard vivaria can be bought assembled or as flat packs for assembly at home. They are less suitable for species requiring higher humidity levels because the moisture eventually seeps into and warps the wood. They are well insulated to keep herps warm with minimum loss of heat. They are functional and stackable but the least aesthetically pleasing of all the options.

Plastic

Several companies produce "pet home" containers, which are stocked by most pet stores. They are useful for rearing juvenile snakes and lizards or for keeping and breeding invertebrates and live foods. They are colorful and cheap, but few are secure or large enough for long-term maintenance of larger snakes and lizards. Unless you can use only a heat pad, few have the potential to fit a spotlight or thermostat. They are especially useful if keeping animals in a room that is already heated. The acrylic material deteriorates with age and is never as clear as glass, but, on the plus side, they are easy to move around and intrinsically safer than glass.

Lighting and heating

In a vivarium, try to provide the correct conditions for your pet to thrive in by providing suitable artificial heat and light. Spotlights are useful for general lighting and provide hot basking spots, which are essential for thermoregulation. When "night" falls after 12–16 hours of "daytime," the temperature of a vivarium may drop significantly without the additional aid of a heater pad.

This glass vivarium is specifically designed for the care of many featured species.

Which lighting is best?

Nocturnal animals are most active in low-light conditions. Crepuscular species, such as toads and geckos, are most active at dawn and dusk, when the light is reduced. Other species, such as the Bearded Dragon and Veiled Chameleon, will sunbathe in brilliant daylight at temperatures of up to 100°F (38°C), but they will still need a nighttime dark period for sleep. The number of daylight hours and length of a season can also be important if you want to breed your pets. Keep all these factors in mind when lighting the vivarium.

must know

Herptiles and thermoregulation

A temperature gradient is essential for the successful maintenance of most herptiles. They thermoregulate, or move between different temperature zones, to warm up or cool down as required. Without adequate warmth, they cannot feed, digest food, or even move about. At different times of the day or night, they will seek an environment that suits their needs, and you must provide these different environmental conditions within the vivarium. A good temperature gradient can be established using a thermostat to control temperature. The chart below shows the effect of temperature on most herptiles. Most prefer a vivarium with temperature zones within the generally preferred range. Keep your animals at their preferred temperature; if it gets too hot or cold, they may suffer or even perish.

	Critically cold			Generally preferred range		Critically hot	
°F	32	37	50	68	95	113	122
°C	0	4	10	20	35	45	50

Full spectrum lighting

Most snakes, invertebrates, and amphibians can, with a good diet and vitamin and mineral supplementation, thrive in captivity once the correct temperature gradient is provided with little need for what are called full spectrum lights. However, many day-active creatures need unfiltered sunlight to grow and develop healthy bones and skeletons. This can be provided artificially by buying full-spectrum lighting, such as. tubes and lamps designed to supply ultraviolet light, or UVA and UVB, like real sunlight. In essence, a full-spectrum light is at the least beneficial, and it is often essential for herptiles that need to bask as well as many diurnal species.

A good selection of light tubes and bulbs are now available, including the self-ballasted Mercury Vapor lamps. It appears that herbivores and omnivores are most at risk of metabolic bone disease (MBD), a condition that develops in some herptiles given inadequate exposure to real or artificial sunlight. Whenever possible, exposure to real sunlight is of huge benefit to all captive reptiles and amphibians.

Equipment

Your choice of pet will dictate what equipment you require to create the right environment. Every animal in this book can be housed successfully using a selection of the equipment described below.

Thermometer

One or more thermometers should be placed strategically near the main heat source and midway towards the cooler end of the vivarium in order to make accurate temperature checks.

Thermometer

Hygrometer

Heater pad

Ceramic heater

Thermostat

Hygrometer
This measures humidity and is a useful addition to any environment that needs regular monitoring.

Heater pads
A good range of low-, medium-, and high-wattage pads are available. Low-wattage pads are ideal for heating invertebrates, or you may use higher wattage pads in conjunction with a thermostat. Never cover more than half the ground area in the vivarium with a heater pad.

Ceramic heaters
These powerful heaters are excellent for creating hotter basking areas for Bearded Dragons and Veiled Chameleons, although they don't provide any light. They must be thermostatically controlled, and pets and keepers must be protected from contact.

Thermostats
These are essential items for the regulation of temperature output of heaters in the vivarium.

Full spectrum tubes and bulbs
A range of products are available to suit the needs of most species. The tubes can provide essential UVA and UVB light and help promote plant health.

Spotlights and lightbulbs
These are useful for heating and lighting, but they have no ultraviolet light content. Vivarium animals and furnishing should be protected from contact with them. For proper heat control, they are best regulated with a thermostat.

Water bowls

Keep these level with, or lower than, the surrounding ground level. You can use almost any suitable-size bowl or jar lid. The manufactured type look more natural and have rough edges to give reptiles a better grip for getting in and out of the water. Keep the bowls clean and replenished with fresh water. Remember that some species prefer large bowls for bathing and others only drink from water droplets.

Hide

Hide rocks and wood

These give herptiles and invertebrates a sense of security, such as a rock to crawl under. It is better to have too many than too few. Terrestrial animals want ground hides, whereas arboreal species prefer higher hides attached to the side of the vivarium. Cork bark is attractive and available in logs that are simple to break into small pieces. Avoid stacking heavy rocks—they may collapse and crush a pet that is digging.

Plastic plant

External and internal power filters

For optimum reptile and amphibian health, water purity is essential. The larger external power filters heat the water and keep it clean and flowing. I can't overstate how important water quality is, especially for semiaquatic or totally aquatic creatures.

Naturalistic backgrounds

Long pictures of natural landscapes are effective for any setup and come in many designs. They can be cut to the required length and simply attached to the outside of a glass vivarium or inside a wooden one. If used inside, be careful when attaching one because adhesive tape can tear a reptile's skin.

Naturalistic background

Depending on the species you choose, many options are available to create the right environment for your pet.

must know

It goes without saying that you should read instructions carefully on all equipment and follow normal electrical safety rules. If in doubt, you should contact a qualified electrician.

Plastic and silk plants

Available in many colors and leaf forms, artificial plants can provide cover, resting and climbing areas, and make a setup look more attractive. They can be washed and disinfected easily. A small pile of plastic plants sprayed with water creates a humid micro-climate appreciated even by desert species, especially when sloughing, and helps stop dehydration. Never site plastic plants and other furnishings too near to any spotlights, lightbulbs, and other heaters. **Caution**: Some herbivorous reptiles will try to eat them and may get sick.

Real plants

These are good for larger vivaria, especially those with full spectrum lighting, which helps plants to thrive. Sturdy plants, such as Philodendron (*Pothos*), are ideal for Chameleons, whereas a spider plant suits

After creating the right environment, this Blue Tongued Skink will thrive in a vivarium.

These artificial shelters provide a safe and secure retreat, which is essential for the well-being of most pet herptiles.

Anolis or other lightweight species. There is no need to plant a nicely arranged setup for larger, more boisterous species, such as the Blue-Tongued Skink or Iguana; they will destroy or flatten your efforts.

Substrates

Many substrates are available, and your choice will depend on the needs of your pet and your

aesthetic preference. For ease of maintenance,
many breeders and herpetologists keep lizards
and snakes in bare, laboratory-style setups with
newspaper as a base. This may not affect the
happiness of the animal at all, but I prefer
naturalistic displays incorporating a mixture of
substrates and furnishings. Listed below are some
popular options, but if the substrate is clean and
free from pests, parasites, or toxins, many natural
items found in your locality—twigs, leaves,
stones, and gravel—can all be safely utilized.

Play sand and pebbles

These are useful for desert species, and a mixture of
sand, pebbles, and wood chips will enhance the

A variety of natural and artificial
material can be used to create a
visually appealing vivarium pet.

design of most vivaria. Some specialty reptile stores sell decorative colored sands for desert-style setups.

Wood or bark chips

A wide variety is available, but avoid the finest types because the particles may be taken in with food, causing digestive problems. This is a common problem with captive lizards, especially juveniles.

Shredded aspen

This is a good choice, because it lets species burrow into it for security, making it ideal for many snakes.

Leaf litter

Attractive seasonal leaves and pine cones, for example, can enhance the appearance of a vivarium. Freeze them first to kill any resident pests.

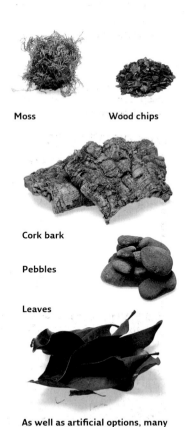

Moss **Wood chips**

Cork bark

Pebbles

Leaves

Reptile grass

This is a green matting that is easily washed and is versatile. It can be placed on the ground, or on the side of the vivarium, for arboreal species.

Paper

Paper is easy to clean and replace but not very pleasing to the eye. Ensure that your vivarium pet is not under-stimulated by a bare or barren vivarium.

Vermiculite

This natural product is excellent when wetted (and any excess moisture squeezed out) for providing an incubating medium for most eggs. It can be used as a substrate for spiders and other vivarium creatures.

As well as artificial options, many natural products are suitable as substrate and decoration.

Feeding your pet

All creatures need food to grow and thrive. Whereas herbivores eat only plant foods, some animals are less specific and eat other animals, insects, plants, and fruit and are known as omnivores. Animals that feed only on insects are insectivores, while those that feed on other animals are classed as carnivores.

A wide variety of both fruit and vegetables will be consumed by many of the featured species.

Successful feeding

You will need to determine which group your pet belongs to and provide it the right selection of foods, in sufficient quantity and quality, to satisfy its needs. Whatever the diet, it should supply that species' requirements in terms of fats, proteins, carbohydrates, vitamins, and minerals. You also need to consider that feeding can be an important behavioral stimulus. Many insect-eating herptiles, for example, spend much of their life hunting for and catching food. Getting the feeding right for each animal is all part of successful pet management.

Herbivores

Many birds, mammals, and invertebrates are herbivores, as are most tortoises and some lizards. Many species supplement their diets with protein when available. Some is unintentionally consumed with plant matter; some intentionally sought.

A wide variety of fruit and vegetables can be store bought, or grown in a pesticide-free vegetable garden. Among the most suitable are lettuce, broccoli, tomato, pear, apple, seasonal berries, such as raspberries and blackberries, dandelion flowers and their leaves and roots, spinach, carrot, cooked potato, cabbage, grasses and nonpoisonous tree leaves, flowers, and seeds.

Many complete foods are also available, as are balanced meals with added vitamins and minerals. Personally, I believe that you can do no better than provide your pet with a range of fresh foodstuffs, but complete foods are handy and not subject to seasonal availability. They are particularly useful if someone is caring for your pet in your absence.

Omnivores

Creatures that feed on plants and other animal species are omnivores—this category includes humans. Omnivores featured in this book, such as the Veiled Chameleon, Bearded Dragon, and Blue-Tongued Skink, will be satisfied with a combination of foods from the herbivore, insectivore, and carnivore sections.

Individual preferences vary but Blue-Tongued Skinks, for example, are usually partial to snails in their shells; an adult specimen will probably enjoy two or three snails and one-quarter of a banana at one sitting. Insects are full of protein and few lizards will pass up the opportunity to eat these nutritious titbits—even those species considered herbivorous.

This Green Anole enjoys both hunting for and consuming its insect prey.

Insectivores

Due to increased interest in keeping and breeding
herptiles, the range, quality, and availability of live
foods has grown greatly over the last few years.
If you cannot obtain foodstuffs from your local pet
store, you may easily purchase them by mail order.
Insectivores, and most omnivores, will enjoy a
selection from the following live foods, which are
listed in order of size.

Locusts (*Locusta migratoria, Schistocerca gregaris*)
The fat-bodied, winged adults are ideal for large
insectivores, although the spiky legs are not always
appreciated. The young are referred to as hoppers.
Usually measuring $1/2$–$1^1/_2$ inches (1–4 cm.), they
are ideal for smaller lizards and frogs. Locusts tend
to climb upward, so are ideal for arboreal species.

Crickets (*Gryllus sp.*)
Probably the most widely available and inexpensive
of all insect foods, these range from pinhead-size
hatchlings to adults over 1 inch (3 cm.) long. Various
species are reared, but I prefer the black, silent
crickets. They are plumper, quieter, and less likely
than the brown-colored house cricket (*Acheta
domestica*) to take up residence in the house if they
escape. The hatchlings are excellent for the tiniest
frog or newly hatched lizard.

Mealworms (*Tenebrio sp and Zophobas sp.*)
Many species find these beetle larvae difficult to
digest. Never use them exclusively, but only as part
of a varied diet. Once they metamorphose into
beetles, most reptiles will refuse to eat them.

**These are the most popular live
foods available to cater for the
needs of your pet.**

Waxworms *(Galleria sp.)*

The larvae of a small moth, these are also edible in adult form. Among the most nutritious and easily digested of live foods, they are useful for building up a weak, ill, or stressed pet. Although excellent to use when taming lizards and frogs, don't feed them too often as they are rich. They are fast movers and will wriggle into tiny nooks and crannies within the vivarium—feeding by hand will prohibit this.

Fruit flies *(Drosophila sp.)*

These little flies suit many baby lizards, frogs, and invertebrates, such as praying mantids. They can be raised on fruit or special culture mixes. Since fruit flies quickly infest a location, you may prefer to order large flightless ones *(Trinidadian sp.)*.

A selection of prepared canned foods is available at most good pet stores.

Other foods

The following foods are suitable for insectivores and omnivores. Some can be collected in the wild, whereas others are aquatic or carnivorous.

Collecting your own

Farmed live foods should be raised in hygienic conditions. One of the problems of collecting your own is that you always run the risk of introducing a parasite or unwanted guest. Having said this, one of the benefits of using wild-caught live foods is that they are packed with naturally acquired vitamins and minerals. They include the following:

• **Snails:** These calcium-rich creatures are liked by Blue-Tongued Skinks, many toads, and small lizards.
• **Worms:** Use earthworms purchased at a reptile store or bred at home from bought varieties. Some

Once thawed, most snakes,
and some lizards, will enjoy
natural "whole foods," such
as these rodents.

species are toxic to amphibians and reptiles, especially
those inhabiting compost piles or rotting vegetation.
• **Spiders:** All spiders have fangs, but most are not
dangerous to humans; adult supervision is advised.
Check the species before collecting.

Aquatic foods

Foods for aquatic amphibians and rearing foods for
animals at larval stages of development can be
purchased from good pet stores. They include:
• **Tubifex:** These red aquatic worms are ideal for
newts, Axolotls, and many animals at the larval/
tadpole stages.
• **Daphnia:** These crustaceans are found in ponds.
• **Brine shrimp** (*Artemia sp.*): These may be bought
alive or as eggs and require a salty solution that
should be filtered before being offered as food.
• **Freshwater shrimp:** These are ideal for Axolotls,
newts, and Oriental Fire-Bellied Toads.
• **Pond pellets and flaked fish foods:** Some
Axolotls and aquatic frogs and newts will readily
accept pellets. Most tadpoles will munch on flaked
fish food, a complete and nutritious foodstuff.

Carnivores

The term "carnivore" is largely used to describe
flesh-eating animals. Within this book, the only true
carnivores are snakes. For most of their lives, snakes
in captivity will accept dead, thawed-out rodents
and are known as "defrost feeders." The rodents
may be purchased prefrozen. For humane reasons,
your pets should not be fed live vertebrate food.
Snakes consume their food whole, so there is no
mess or leftovers, and it would seem that their

vitamin and mineral requirements are met by their small rodent diet. Supplements are not generally needed, although you may add vitamin drops to the snake's water occasionally. Rodents fed include:

• **Mice** *(Mus musculus)*: These are the best and most popular foodstuff for snakes. Juvenile, hairless mice, called pinkies, are an ideal size for hatchlings and juvenile snakes. Fuzzies, juvenile haired mice, are the next size up. Purchase them prefrozen from your pet store or specialty herpetological supplier.

• **Rats** *(Rattus)*: Small and medium-size rats, preferably brown or black in color, are a good-size food for Ball Pythons and larger Kingsnakes.

• **Other rodents:** Many smaller rodents are accepted by a variety of snakes—gerbils are particularly favored by Ball Pythons. All frozen rodents should be fed to your pet only once they are thawed and warmed. Should you breed your own, rodents must be kept and then killed in a humane way.

Feeding snakes

Some processed snake foods are now available, but they are more expensive than rodents and I don't think they are necessary. Many species prefer to feed at dawn or dusk, or at least in low-light conditions. Offer your pet a thawed-out rodent held by its tail, using long tweezers. It should be accepted readily if a snake is hungry and not nervous. For many snakes, especially juveniles, leave the food in a hide box overnight, where the snake can find it at its leisure and then consume it in peace. Uneaten food should be removed and disposed of—do not refreeze it.

Conveniently for the pet keeper, snakes consume their food whole and there is no mess.

Sometimes a bit of variety in the diet helps. This Axolotl enjoys the occasional earthworm.

Supplements

A range of products are now available for herptiles. The most important ones for many species contain added vitamins and minerals. Some new products claim to provide the UVA and UVB requirements of basking species in a liquid form. Use all products in moderation and at the recommended dose.

Feeding tips

Some people prefer to feed their pet in a separate container to the one in which it lives. Plastic pet homes are ideal and can also be used to keep your live foods. With this method, it may be easier to monitor how much is eaten by each pet. It may also train your pet to accept being handled first before receiving its food reward in its feeding box. It is important to keep and breed your live foods in hygienic and humane conditions. Care instructions should be available from your supplier or pet center.

When pets refuse to feed

Species can stop feeding for many reasons. If you have had your pet for a while, it is likely that it is well fed, with built-up fat reserves, and is "full." After a short break (a few days for a lizard to several months for a snake) it will continue to feed normally, so do not worry if it refuses food occasionally. However, there are times when you should be concerned about lack of appetite, such as:

• If you have just acquired it, and it has not eaten at all within the first week or so.

• It is getting thin or weak, or becoming less active. If your pet is not eating, then check the following:

• Have you created the right environment? Is the unit warm enough or too warm? Is there enough water?

• Have you offered foods of the right type and size? Is the live food hassling your pet? Is the food offered in the right place and at the right time of day?

• Is your pet sloughing? Most species will refuse foods at this time but are hungry again afterward.

Praying Mantids enjoy hunting live insect prey and prefer insects that will climb up onto twigs and branches in their vivarium.

Health and preventative care

Most health problems can be prevented, since the major cause of herptile ill health is poor husbandry or injury caused by you or another animal. By providing the correct environment, which is hygienically maintained, with the right quantity and quality of foods, most health problems can be prevented easily.

must know

Vitamin and mineral supplements are essential for many species. Give the correct dosage, because a lack, or excess, of vitamins and minerals can lead to health problems. They are important for juveniles that are developing quickly. Always be sure to follow the manufacturers' guidelines.

Buying healthy specimens

I recommend that novices purchase captive-bred specimens wherever possible. Imported, wild-caught species are more likely to have internal and external parasites and bacterial infections. Many of these problems can be overcome with correct medication and laboratory-style/quarantine housing. Contact your specialty society or dealer for advice if you think your pet has problems of this nature. If you think your pet is sick or suffering, contact a herptile-proficient veterinarian immediately.

Obesity

Obesity is a major health risk for all pets. Too much food or a diet too high in preferred or fatty foods can cause serious problems. It is impossible to state exactly what quantity of each foodstuff should be given to any species, but try to imagine life in the wild where most would not eat every day or all-year round. Encourage activity in predatory herptiles by scattering food—this makes your animal "work" for its meal. Dragging a defrosted mouse around the vivarium using long tweezers for a snake or releasing some bugs into the vivarium for a Leopard Gecko to physically stalk will aid this type of positive "exercise."

Metabolic bone disease

This is common in some species of captive-bred reptiles. Without exposure to UVB rays, they cannot synthesize Vitamin D3, which they need to absorb calcium to form healthy bones. There are a variety of products available, and I would advise using a fluorescent full-spectrum tube, with both UVA and UVB, or giving a powdered Vitamin D3 supplement.

Abscesses

Common in snakes and lizards, these may appear as a raised bump underneath the scales. A veterinarian can surgically remove the infected swelling and cleanse and suture the wound afterward.

Dehydration

The symptoms of dehydration are sunken eyes and remnants of unsuccessfully shed skin still attached to the body. Mild cases can be treated by improving your pet's vivarium conditions. Mist spray and make sure the animal drinks. Water bowls can be sunk into the substrate to ground level for ease of access. However, bad cases need veterinarian treatment.

Some moist moss or plants inside this "hide" assist snakes when they are due to shed their skin by allowing them access to increased humidity.

Improved water quality may have prevented the infection that led to the loss of an eye in this frog.

Sloughing

Maintaining the right humidity levels is key in preventing problems when sloughing. The inability to remove old skin properly can result in a restricted blood supply, especially to blood vessels around toes and fingers. A humidity chamber—a box containing well sprayed plastic plants—is helpful in many species and provides objects for them to rub against to aid the slough. Common problems include:

• A spectacle remaining on a snake—this can be removed carefully with moisture and tweezers by an experienced herpetologist.

• Tattered sloughing in a snake or lizard due to inadequate humidity.

External parasites

These are common problems for reptiles. Mites are pinheadlike objects that run about a reptile's scales, while ticks burrow under the scales, especially near the eyes, nostrils, or vent. Good hygiene can help to prevent the problem. Control external parasites with products containing permethrin. Disinfect the vivarium and furnishings, wash the reptile, and treat according to the instructions on the packaging. **Caution:** These products may harm or kill any invertebrate or aquatic animals.

Blisters

These are especially common on Garter Snakes and other species of moist habitats due to the vivarium substrate being too wet or inadequately ventilated. Blisters are also caused by the larvae of nematodes (wormlike parasites). Veterinary treatment is recommended using antiseptic or antibiotics.

Ingested substrate

This causes major problems for many herptiles. Avoid it by providing food in dishes and ensuring feeding animals do not take in any substrate with their food.

Bacterial infections

These are most common in amphibians because of their delicate skin and aquatic lifestyles. Good water quality is essential—external or internal filtration is the most effective tool in preventing infection. Regularly remove dead foodstuffs and fecal matter by hand or a net. Water bowls must be cleaned and changed, so fresh water is always available.

Salmonellosis

Salmonellosis is an infection caused by contact with the bacteria salmonella. These tiny organisms or germs pass from the feces of animals or people to other people, foods, or animals and cause sickness. Salmonellosis causes diarrhea, abdominal pains, or fever and is usually short-lived, but children and the elderly are susceptible, and it can become a serious health condition requiring antibiotic treatment.

As well as being found in uncooked meats and eggs, salmonella germs are common in pet animals, such as birds and reptiles. If you heed normal animal/human hygiene procedures, such as washing hands with a microbacterial solution, never cleaning animal housing or equipment in the same area used for food preparation, and disinfecting equipment on a regular basis, you have little to worry about. All pets should be kept clean and away from kitchens. After any contact with an animal, wash your hands.

want to know more?

• A specialty herptile supplier should be able to give detailed advice and be knowledgeable about the equipment required to care for these unusual pets. A good store will stock a wide selection of equipment.
• By using the Internet or your local telephone book, you should be able to find a supplier near to where you live.

2 Amphibians

Frogs and other amphibians are probably the most colorful pets it is possible to keep. Many hours can be spent watching their behavior, from the seemingly smiling tree frogs to the antics of an Axolotl or the stalking of a worm by a newt. The vivarium they live in can be planted or otherwise decorated to become a fascinating and attractive feature of any household. Many are kept purely to be enjoyed aesthetically, but others are easy and safe to handle. Keeping any pet has its responsibilities, but amphibians are relatively straightforward to care for, with remarkably simple requirements. They do not need much in the way of day-to-day attention and they can be a joy for their owner.

What are amphibians?

Amphibians ruled the earth before any reptiles, birds, or mammals even existed. The word amphibian is derived from the Greek words *amphi*, meaning "both," and *bios*, meaning "life." Amphibians are suited to life on land and in the water and usually have a two-stage life cycle, starting out as aquatic and moving to life on land.

must know

Many amphibians are bred in captivity as pets every year, greatly improving the quality of animals available. Buying a captive-reared juvenile is the best way for you to start keeping, learning about, and enjoying these varied, fascinating creatures. A captive-bred frog or salamander will already be adapted to life in a vivarium and more easily conditioned to handling by humans.

Ectotherms

Amphibians have a delicate, moist skin with a protective mucus covering. They slough this periodically, and it is generally eaten. Many display wonderful colors, either for camouflage or as a warning to potential predators to show that they possess toxic skins. Amphibians are ectotherms and are entirely reliant on environmental warmth to maintain their body functions. Most species from temperate climates hibernate in winter to avoid lethally cold temperatures. Species from tropical climates estivate (pass the summer in a dormant state). Fortunately, in captivity, we can control the environmental conditions, so that they are more suited to year-round activity.

Vertebrates

All amphibians are vertebrates with a complete skeleton from the skull down to tiny toe bones. As adults, all are predators, feeding mainly on spiders and insects, although larger species will consume small reptiles and mammals. Foods are swallowed rather than chewed. To aid this process, frogs, for example, have tiny peglike teeth to hold the prey before it is swallowed.

Reproduction

Amphibians generally lay soft, jelly-covered eggs in water. Depending on the species, these are usually laid in clumps or strings, although some deposit their eggs elsewhere, such as on leaves overhanging a pond. Thousands may be laid by each individual, and millions, when frogs, congregate to breed en masse. However, mortality is high and fewer than one percent in the wild are likely to reach maturity. The eggs usually hatch into larvae (tadpoles), which, after taking on nutrients, undergo a shape-changing metamorphosis into adult form. They then leave the water and adopt a more terrestrial lifestyle.

The skeleton is the internal frame for all amphibians, and it helps to protect their major organs.

Axolotl *Ambystoma mexicanum*

Found in the wild only in the canal system of the former Lake Xochimilcho in Mexico, these strange amphibians are easy to keep and make attractive, if unusual, aquatic pets. Although officially an endangered species, Axolotls have been available from captive-bred stock since the 1830s.

must know

The Axolotl has been much studied due to its amazing powers of regeneration. A lost or damaged limb will regrow over a period of about eight weeks. The new limb will be just as good as the old one and full flexibility will be retained. However, occasionally, due to the extent of the original injury, the regenerated limb may regrow at an unusual angle.

Appearance

Black or dark gray is the most common coloring, but albino, harlequin, and, more recently, a golden form have all been captive bred and are available to the pet keeper. Growing to 12 inches (30 cm.), an Axolotl should live 10–12 years in captivity, although older specimens of some 20 years have been reported.

Neotony

An unusual feature of Axolotls is that they do not go through a normal amphibian life cycle in which eggs laid in water by the adult hatch into tadpolelike "larvae" and then metamorphose into adults. At this stage, the animal frequently leaves the water to take up a more terrestrial lifestyle. Axolotls have foregone the need to undergo metamorphosis. They remain in the aquatic larval stage and reproduce without the need to become adult—this is called neotony.

An Axolotl can only change into adult form when the hormone thyroxine is introduced into its diet or there is an increase in the iodine levels in the water. The Axolotl gradually loses its external gills, the tail reduces, and, upon leaving the water, it becomes a Mexican Salamander. Metamorphosis will not normally take place without this special treatment.

Creating the right environment

A perfect home for a single axolotl is an aquarium measuring 24 x 15 x 12 inches (60 x 38 x 30 cm.). Make sure that the water is roughly neutral (pH 6.5–7.5) and is maintained at a temperature of between 50°F (10°C) and 77°F (25°C)—a heater is not usually required. Water depth can be at least as deep as the length of your Axolotl, but specimens missing a limb or two may prefer shallower water until these have fully regenerated.

Axolotls will soon ruin a delicately planted aquarium, so they are best kept in a plain setup or with some sturdier aquarium/pond plants. Gravel, pebbles, and even fine sand are all suitable substrates. Adding larger rocks will provide visual appeal to the aquarium and will give your Axolotl some platforms upon which to rest. An external or

The long and feathery external gills allow the Axolotl to obtain the oxygen it needs.

This black Axolotl is being carefully lifted to enable its aquarium to be cleaned.

internal filter is recommended to clean and aerate the water but it is not essential. Weekly cleaning of furnishings and partial changes of water is acceptable, although a time-consuming, alternative.

Generally speaking, Axolotls are best housed separately because they have a tendency to eat each other's limbs. Don't worry if this happens—they do regrow eventually, if not as perfectly as their originals. Keeping these creatures separately does not usually cause problems, because they seem totally unconcerned about the lack of company.

Handling

Axolotls are aquatic animals and do not like frequent handling. When necessary, they can be moved by scooping them into a net or by gently cradling them in the hands. Always transfer them between waters of similar age and temperature to avoid causing a shock.

Feeding

Axolotls are predators and will eat a large range of foods. Worms, crickets, small fish, fish pellets that sink or float, cubes of heart or lean meat are suitable foodstuffs. Keep food pieces to small, mouth-size chunks because Axolotls cannot chew.

A young Axolotl needs "training" to learn how to catch nonmoving food, and long tweezers can be used to drop a piece of food onto its face. They suck their prey in, and this violent motion can scare you from using your own fingers, but their teeth are fine and will not hurt the more adventurous keeper willing to hold a piece of food between finger and thumb. Axolotls can be fed every other day, with several mouthfuls of food given per sitting. Hungry Axolotls do seem to patrol their environment more than their well-fed companions—an indication that more food may be required. Uneaten food should be removed as soon as possible to minimize fouling.

Breeding

Once your pet is two years old, the sexes can be distinguished easily. Viewed from above, the male Axolotl's head is longer and narrower than the female's, his tail is longer, and the swelling at the cloaca is greater.

In captivity, the breeding season coincides with a change of temperature. This can be induced artificially by raising the water temperature to 72°F (22°C) for about a week, and then letting it drop quickly. With luck and a good diet, breeding behavior should follow. The female will become attracted to the male's scent, follow him around the aquarium, and they dance and swim around one another for some time. Eventually, the male releases triangular jelly masses, called spermatophores, that sink to the bottom of the aquarium. The female is led over these masses until she takes some up into her cloacal opening. Some hours later she will start to spawn, and 300–600 fertilized eggs are laid.

The egg masses are best reared separately from the parents to prevent them from being damaged or eaten. The eggs need good aeration from a pump. After about two weeks at 68°F (20°C), the larvae will hatch and can then be fed on brine shrimp, tubifex, powdered fish food, or other microscopic foods. As they grow, daphnia, glassworms, bloodworms, and mosquito larvae can also be consumed.

must know

When decorating an aquarium for aquatic amphibians, it is important to select rocks, gravel, and other furnishings that are suitable from a pet store. Some rocks, stones, or pieces of wood found in your yard may, in fact, be toxic or too sharp for safe use.

Red-Spotted Newt *Notophthalmus viridescens*

Native to Eastern North America, these charming and attractive newts make an ideal introduction for novices to the world of tailed amphibians. Easy to maintain, they will grow to a length of 4 inches (10 cm.) and live for four to six years.

must know

Red-Spotted Newts go through a "red eft" stage upon metamorphosis. These juveniles are usually red with black dots on their backs and lead a terrestrial lifestyle for two to three years. Once adult, their skin is brown and covered in red spots encircled with a black border. At this stage, they return to the water to live and breed.

These small, attractive newts are easy to keep as pets.

Creating the right environment

The habitat requirements of these newts change as they mature. Metamorphosed juveniles are terrestrial, but adults are mostly aquatic. Several newts may be accommodated in a 24 x 15 x 12-inch (60 x 38 x 30-cm.) aquarium, but a larger unit will give you more scope to create a semiaquatic setup for both stages of the life cycle.

A well-planned vivarium consists of a densely planted aquatic region, with a water depth of about 6–9 inches (15–23 cm.), and a large platform or cork logs to create a land area. Some sloping branches or rocks provide easy access to the water.

Cover the land area with leaf litter, moss, and wood chips to create shelter for both living and hunting. These creatures do not want their habitat to become either too dry or too damp, so aim for humidity of around 40–50 percent. Fluorescent lighting would help the overall appearance and also ensure that the plants grow. Do not heat the aquarium—this is important because these newts are content to live with a room temperature of 65°F (18°C) and no higher than 72°F (22°C). An aquarium filter will help maintain good water quality.

Handling

Red-Spotted Newts produce toxic skin secretions, making them unpalatable to many predators. Although these toxins will not make you ill, it is always advisable to handle your newts as little as possible. If you do need to handle them, be careful because they are small and easily injured.

Your pet newt will enjoy hunting for food both above and below the surface of the water.

Feeding

Terrestrial efts will hunt small live foods, such as young crickets, waxmoth, fruit flies, worms, and spiders. Aquatic adults will hunt daphnia, mosquito larvae, and bloodworm, but will also take small food items from the surface of the water. Leave some live foods in the aquarium to allow the newts to hunt at will—but do not overwhelm them.

Breeding

Male Red-Spotted Newts actively court the females in the water during springtime. A few weeks after a successful pairing, the female newt will lay up to 400 individual eggs in the aquarium. These will hatch in four to eight weeks, and the tiny larvae begin to feed on suspended microorganisms for about three months. During this time, they will grow from $1/2$ inch (1 cm.) to 2 inches (4.5 cm.) in length and will be ready to undergo their shape-changing metamorphosis.

Paddle-Tailed Newt *Pachytriton labiatus*

Paddle Tails are an interesting, predatory, tailed amphibian from parts of southern China. Rubbery, chubby, and chocolate brown with a bright red streaky belly and flat head, they are appealing newts. They have a broad, flattened paddle of a tail to help them navigate the fast-flowing streams that make up their habitat in the wild.

must know

Invisible scents called pheromones are produced by the male's cloacal glands, and waft toward a potential mate, using the tail. A receptive female will be attracted toward the male, who deposits a jellylike package of sperm (spermatophore). Eventually, often after an elaborate courtship dance, the female will pick up the deposited package directly into her cloacal region.

Creating the right environment

A covered aquarium that is 36 x 15 x 12 inches (90 x 38 x 30 cm) with some floating "land" areas is ideal for a small group of these territorial amphibians. Rocks, real and otherwise, should be utilized to provide multiple hiding and hunting areas for these aggressive creatures. A power filter should be considered essential for water purity and to create a current of moving water around the aquarium. Water temperature should remain cool at about 60°F (15°C), so heating is not required. However, a full-spectrum light will be helpful for plants and will illuminate the aquarium during the day without raising the water temperature.

Handling

It is best not to pick up these animals but to move them by net or transport them in a small, water-filled fish bag or a moss-filled container. They do breathe air but spend most of their time submerged, coming to the surface of the water only to gulp air or snap at prey.

Feeding

As predators, these newts prefer to hunt living prey around the aquarium; aquatic foods, such as tubifex, blood worm, whiteworm, or little freshwater shrimp, are ideal. Small fish, earthworms, crickets, slugs, and maggots can all be tried. Variety is important, and any uneaten foods should be removed to minimize fouling the aquatic environment. Paddle Tails are little water tigers and will suck in and try to eat whatever takes their fancy.

Newts make fascinating, low-cost pets and their aquarium can be decorated to enhance any room.

Breeding

This is not a species that is widely bred in captivity but it can be achieved if you persist, with good general care of your newts. Males, when in breeding condition, develop several bold white spots on the tail and can usually be identified by their swollen cloaca. Females can lay 40–50 large ¼ inch (4–5 mm.) eggs a season, which stick to the sides of rocks or caverns. These should hatch after about eight weeks and, if well fed, the tadpoles metamorphose at two to three months. They may at this stage require a more mossy, land area than a totally aquatic environment.

The rocks and plants in this aquarium have created the ideal environment for a Paddle-Tailed Newt. It has plenty of places to hide and can climb out of the water if it chooses to do so.

Fire Salamander *Salamandra salamandra*

These secretive creatures are mainly nocturnal, hidden under rocks or inside old rodent burrows during the day. Their natural range extends through central and southern Europe into North Africa and Western Asia. Their bright yellow coloration on an oily black skin is striking; they grow up to 12 inches (30 cm.) long.

must know

Fire Salamanders, like some other amphibians, are very visually aware and will set up "home" at a regular site. When cleaning out the vivaria, replace some "landmark" objects in their original spots to avoid confusing your pets.

Creating the right environment

Fire Salamanders are easy enough to keep but as territorial creatures they are best housed individually. A 36 x 15 x 12-inch (90 x 38 x 30-cm.) vivarium is spacious for a single animal and sufficient for a pair. Furnish the vivarium with a few inches of peat, moss, and leaves to provide a cool, damp base, and add some cork, a small rotting log, or something similar to provide hiding spaces. A shallow dish sunk into the ground is useful, but, because salamanders drown easily, keep it shallow to ensure that your pet can climb out easily. Mist spray your salamanders regularly. Keep them cool at 60–68°F (15–20°C) in low light conditions; supplementary heating or lighting is usually not required.

Handling

The bright colors of the salamander serve as a warning to potential predators. Many creatures learn quickly that these amphibians ooze toxic, milky secretions from their skin when they are bitten or aggravated. Be particularly careful when handling your pet—enjoy your salamander but treat it with respect. A basic hygiene precaution is to wash your hands after touching any animal.

Feeding

If fed at a regular time, your salamander will learn to emerge from hiding in anticipation of food. These terrestrial amphibians eat a range of slow-moving, ground-living live foods, such as slugs, spiders, and worms. Be careful when you are feeding several salamanders at once. They are quick to snap and are likely to fight over the same worm or cricket. As a simple rule, you should feed your pet salamander only as much as will be eaten at a single sitting, two or three times per week. Without distressing your salamanders too much by leaving excess live food crawling all over them, leave a few worms and insects loose in the vivarium to be eaten or found at their leisure.

Breeding

Fire Salamanders are frequently bred in captivity, during spring and early summer. Courtship occurs on land and involves the male carrying the female, often for several hours, on his back. After stimulation of her cloacal region, the female will pick up a deposited spermatophore. At this time, she needs access to shallow water. She will eventually bear up to 70 well-formed larvae direct into the water.

Unlike frogs, all salamanders and newts are deaf and silent, unable to hear, croak, or call.

African Clawed Frog *Xenopus laevis*

These amphibians are totally aquatic and are notable for the absence of a tongue and eyelids. Their bodies appear somewhat flattened and they possess powerful hind limbs. They are native to southern Africa and grow to approximately 4–5 inches (10–13 cm.). They can live for up to 15 years in captivity.

must know

Clawed frogs really enjoy a variety of foods. You must be careful to ensure your *Xenopus* remains active and fit by eating only enough food to maintain good health. They are prone to obesity and, by overeating, will become unhealthy and have a shorter life span.

Creating the right environment

Simple to maintain in captivity, a 36 x 15 x 12-inch (90 x 38 x 30-cm.) aquarium, half filled, is adequate for a pair of frogs. Ideally, the frogs should be able to reach the surface of the water while standing on the bottom of the tank. Keep the water temperature between 68–77°F (20–25°C) with an aquarium heater, making sure that it is adequately protected from damage by these boisterous frogs. To maintain water purity, gentle filtration, using either internal or external power filters, is essential.

To furnish your setup, you can use plants, rocks, pea-size gravel, or even sturdy plants to allow your frogs places to feel secure. A hiding space, such as a plastic pipe, would be much appreciated. Initially, your pets may bash around a bit, but they will acclimatize well once familiarized with their new surroundings. Make sure you keep a lid firmly on the aquarium to prevent escapes.

Handling

These frogs are difficult to handle. Coated with a protected slime, they can easily slip through your fingers. If you need to move them, catch them in a net and transport them in a plastic container, without water, furnished with wet moss or foam pieces to keep them moist. Do not place them in a bag—remember that their claws are sharp and they may rip the bag to pieces.

Feeding

Healthy *Xenopus*, pronounced "Zenopus", will rarely refuse food, which they shuffle about with their long fingers. They will happily swim to the surface to take food from your fingers, which they will then consume underwater. Earthworms, small fish, waxworms, even turtle and fish food pellets are all agreeable to these frogs.

You should feed only as much as will be eaten in a 10-minute sitting every other day or so. Naturally plump looking, these frogs are prone to gluttony, so keep them healthy.

Breeding

Males and females are easy to tell apart, the female being larger, more rounded, and, when viewed from above, having three visible flaps of skin next to the cloaca. Some environmental changes seem to trigger spawning, and spraying the water surface or adding 2–3 inches (5–8 cm.) of water can start the process. On average, about 1,000 eggs are laid per spawning, and a single female can produce up to 10,000 a season. These should be removed immediately—to prevent the adult frogs eating them—and should be kept in a shallow container until they hatch a couple of days later. The tadpoles will need an organic soup of microscopic foods that they can suck up. Fish fry food and, indeed, specialty *Xenopus* larvae foods are available.

The African Clawed Frog, although unusual and bizarre looking, is actually one of the simplest of all amphibians to keep and maintain successfully in the home.

Oriental Fire-Bellied Toad *Bombina orientalis*

Splashing around the mountain streams and ponds of Russia, China, and Korea is one of the world's most attractive toads. These small, brightly colored amphibians are active, beautifully marked, and easy to care for. Growing to around 2 inches (5cm), these charming little creatures can live for up to 20 years.

must know

Oriental Fire-Bellied Toads have a bright mossy green back speckled with inky black dots and dashes for camouflage, while their underside is an alarmingly reddish orange, warning of their toxicity to predators.

Creating the right environment

An aquarium/vivarium divided into half land, half water suits these toads. The water part, to a depth of, say, 6 inches (15 cm.), can be warmed using an aquarium heater to around 74-77°F (23-25°C); if you live in a colder climate, use a fluorescent light for brightness or a small spotlight. The land area, which needs to be easily reached from the water with branches or rocks helping the toads to climb, should be a moist woodland-type setup with moss, wood chips, and leaves for decoration. Alternatively, just keep them in a woodland-type vivarium with a large water bowl. As a semiaquatic species, water quality is important.

Active during the day, and small and easy to keep, these entertaining toads make ideal pets.

Handling

Handling these toads is safe but not recommended or, indeed, necessary. Like some other amphibians, Oriental Fire-Bellied Toads contain toxins and you should not handle them if you have cuts on your skin. As pets, they are friendly and the release of toxins is rarely seen, so don't let this deter you from keeping these delightful toads.

Feeding

These little toads will feed well on live insect prey. They feed mainly on land and will learn to come to your fingers when offered food. Feed as much as they can eat two to three times a week, adding some vitamin supplements regularly. The superb coloration of Oriental Fire Bellies will fade with captive-bred offspring unless coloring agents are provided (found in prepared fish foods and flakes). The toads can obtain these naturally in the wild by eating a multitude of tiny creatures.

Breeding

Spring is the most likely time for these toads to start calling. The male is noisy and his constant croaking should attract a willing female. Spawning will occur within 8 to 24 hours of mating, probably at night. Up to 200 eggs may be produced singularly or in clumps. Eggs should be removed to a rearing container with similarly aged and warmed water. The $\frac{1}{25}$ inch (2 mm.) eggs hatch a few days later. Once the larvae have absorbed their egg sacks, they will start to eat tiny chopped fish foods and be ready to leave the water (metamorphose) after three weeks as tiny but fully formed toads.

These toads can even be kept communally – a 36 x 15 x 12-inch (90 x 38 x 30-cm.) aquarium is ample for three or four individuals (one male to three females). Security is essential, as they are excellent escapees.

must know

When threatened, these toads first press their belly to the ground and curl their toes and chins upward, flashing their bright red undersides to warn of their toxicity. Should you persist in hassling them, they will flip over, exposing the entire red-and-black belly to deter predators and make themselves appear unpalatable. They can ooze an acrid white fluid from pores on their backs if put under greater stress.

American Green Toad *Bufo debilis*

American Green Toads are attractive with greenish yellow metallic-looking skin, interlaced with jet black dots and dashes, offering superb camouflage in their natural habitat. Native to arid areas of North America, they are small, squat, and undemanding, rarely longer than 2 inches (5 cm.) and widely available in pet stores.

must know

Toads are seemingly more intelligent that most other amphibians and, after a period of adjustment to their new home, many soon become tame and comfortable in your presence. In fact, on seeing you approach the vivarium, they will probably to crawl forward in anticipation of whatever tasty treat you may be about to provide.

Creating the right environment

American Green Toads can be kept in pairs or larger groups, provided that ample resting/hiding areas are provided—cork logs and reptile hides are ideal. These toads will thrive in a 24 x 12 x 12-inch (60 x 30 x 30-cm) vivarium with good ventilation and a substrate of compost or sandy soil to a depth of 3 inches (8 cm.) or so, becaue they like to dig, covered with leaf litter or moss. A shallow water dish should be available and, although they like a dry woodland-type setup, occasional mist spraying is beneficial and encourages foraging activity.

They thrive in a 68–75°F (20–24°C) temperature range; a heater pad may be useful as back up, or a small spot bulb at one end of a larger vivarium gives toads the option to bask and warm up. A fluorescent light will illuminate the vivarium if required during the day without heating the cage, but ensure that the toads have plenty of shady areas or they may remain hidden until nightfall.

Handling

Toads, as a rule, do not enjoy being handled much and are usually kept by people preferring to marvel at their behavior, habits, and aesthetic appeal.

Feeding

While mainly nocturnal, these and many other toad species thrive in low-light conditions but are likely to become day active (diurnal) once they settle into captivity. They will eat most small live foods that are available from pet stores, including small crickets and small worms.

Breeding

Male American toads have dark gray throats and, in the breeding season, nuptial pads (small dark gripping bumps) on the first digit of the front legs. Females are usually larger with a creamy yellow throat and belly. Native to arid plains and grasslands, these tiny toads breed in the temporary pools of water that are found only after rainfall. Both the eggs and tadpoles develop quickly to ensure survival once the pools have dried up. In captivity, significant space and effort will be required if you are raising tadpoles into healthy toadlets.

must know

Toads have enlarged glands behind the head that can secrete a white fluid poison to protect them from predators. This may inflame the mouth, cause nausea, severe irritation, and even death to any aggressor. When handling any species of toad, be careful, although pet toads are unlikely to release the poison.

This attractive little toad is secretive but becomes less shy once settled into its vivarium.

Couch's Spadefoot Toad *Scaphiopus couchii*

With large golden eyes, rounded features, yellow to green markings, and a creamy white belly, Couch's Spadefoot Toad is an attractive little creature, reaching only 2–4 inches (5–9 cm.) in length. These nocturnal, rotund little amphibians live for around 13 years.

must know

Spadefoot Toads like to dig and, using a special spadelike structure on each hind limb, create burrows by shuffling backward into sandy earth. They rest in these burrows and estivate in them during the harsh months. Couch's Spadefoot is found in the southwestern United States into Mexico and the Baja peninsula.

Creating the right environment

A vivarium measuring about 18 x 12 x 12 inches (46 x 30 x 30 cm.), or larger if keeping several toads together, will suffice, with a 4-6-inch (10-15-cm.) deep substrate of semidry sandy soil. Try a 50-50 mix of soil and sand for good burrowing options, although a couple of cavelike retreats on the surface may be preferred. A shallow water dish should always be available. The spotlight or heater pad, controlled by a thermostat, should warm these amphibians to 77–82°F (25–28°C). By using a well ventilated vivarium, an occasional mist spraying will ensure that the toads are warm but do not bake or desiccate in their burrows.

Feeding

Small insects are the preferred diet of these little toads, which eat well but may refuse foods for lengthy periods of time. Wild populations reportedly may not eat for eight to ten months of the year, then feast and breed during the short rainy season. These toads are not particuly active, which, no doubt, assists in keeping them plump with plenty of stored fat. Small crickets are ideal food, but other little live foods should also be offered, such as mini mealworms, waxmoths, and earthworms.

Handling

Spadefoot Toads are not good creatures for handling, and some reports suggest that their skin secretions can cause irritation to human skin. If you do need to pick one up, such as when you are cleaning out the vivarium, always use wet hands to cup the toad and then move it to a temporary container.

Breeding

During the short, warm rainy season, these toads emerge, and the male's sheeplike bleating call will attract females to the temporary shallow pools of water. Eggs are rapidly deposited and hatch within 36 hours. The tadpoles develop incredibly quickly and can metamorphose within seven to eight days, leaving the water as toadlets before the pool dries up. Tadpoles feed on tiny algae, other tadpoles, and undeveloped eggs. If you're breeding them in captivity, the toadlets need to be fed tiny crickets and other nutritious insects in order for them to develop into healthy adults.

Although this is a characterful little toad, it is not a species that is recommended for regular handling by pet owners.

Argentinean Horned Frog
Ceratophrys ornate

These strange-looking, spectacularly colored frogs are native to the warm, swampy forest floor of Argentina, Brazil, Paraguay, and Uruguay. They are variably blotched with mossy greens, yellows, and brown pigments, with prominent raised "horns" behind and above each eye.

must know

An inactive frog with dumpy short legs, it easily spends much of its life burrowed into leaf litter and moss, waiting for the next meal to wander by. Horned Frogs are largely diurnal (day active) as pets and grow to 6 inches (15 cm.), living usually for 6 to 8 years, although 15 years has been recorded.

Creating the right environment

Simple to keep, provided that they are kept warm at around 77–82°F (25–28°C) in a setup that can be cleaned easily, these frogs eat well and excrete a lot. They need a mixture of compost/leaf litter with lots of moss for burrowing. This will need regular changing, so keep it simple to maintain good hygiene. A very shallow water dish is essential—the frogs cannot swim—and they may well sit in it for considerable periods of time. Although they are not good pets for someone wanting to watch agile amphibians on the prowl, they are delightful but lazy slobs. They must be kept alone because they are cannibalistic, territorial, and pugnacious.

This giant of a frog is wonderfully colorful and seemingly always hungry. It makes a hardy, although inactive, pet.

Handling

This is not a frog to be handled—adults can give you a painful bite, and at any age they will try to eat almost anything that moves. Be warned!

Feeding

Horned Frogs are little more than a stomach on legs and tend to try to eat anything and everything that comes close, including your fingers. This is a frog with an incredible appetite, and, as it grows, more food should be offered. Juveniles will invariably eat crickets, but worms, flies, and even small pinkie mice will be accepted. Adults are capable of eating other frogs, lizards, snakes, and rodents, but, apart from the odd mouse every eight to ten days, most people give them big crickets, worms, and locusts. Dead foods are likely to be taken only if wriggled around on long tweezers.

An ambush predator with good camouflage, the Horned Frog will sit and wait patiently for potential food to come toward it.

Breeding

Easy to keep, these frogs thrive in captivity and many are bred in a range of colors. Reaching sexual maturity at two to three years of age, breeding is initiated by the smaller darker males calling for the colorful females during the rainy season. From 300 to 1,000 eggs are deposited on fake or real plants in a shallow water puddle. These hatch within a week or so and require considerable space, filtration, and effort to keep them well fed on earthworm, blood worm, and tubifex. The tadpoles are carnivorous, aggressive, and will attack and eat each other as well as small fish. They metamorphose within 30 days into tiny $^1/_2$-inch (1–1.3-cm.) froglets, which are also happy to eat each other.

must know

As well as relying on its camouflage for hunting, this frog uses an amazing technique called "pedal luring" to actively entice food items to venture close. Pedal luring involves wriggling one or more toes to look like a worm, so unsuspecting prey are lured into range of the Horned Frog's cavernous mouth.

Australian Green Tree Frog *Litoria caerulea*

This wonderful, large green chubby, smiling frog is the most suitable tree frog for the pet keeper. Native to New Guinea and much of Northern and Eastern Australia, they prefer forest but are also common around human habitation. Reaching 2–4 inches (5–10 cm.) in length, they live for about 15 years.

These wonderfully robust tree frogs are the easiest to handle amphibian in this book and probably the most popular pet frog in the world.

Creating the right environment

Tall vivaria are required for most tree frogs and these are no exception. A vivarium that measures 24 x 18 x 12 inches (60 x 45 x 30 cm.) and is decorated with a branch, plants, or logs is ideal for a few frogs. A substrate of moss, bark chips, or pebbles is recommended, but a barer base is sufficient and will be much easier to clean.

A large bowl of water should always be offered, and a daily mist spraying is beneficial for the frogs. However, make sure there is a reasonable amount of ventilation to prevent excess dampness. Keep the temperature at 77–86°F (25–30°C) during the day and reduce slightly at night. Only keep similarly sized animals together.

Handling

Australian Tree Frogs are very easy to handle. They climb and stick to your hands well, but they may at times leap or jump. When they are first held, they may expel some liquid from their anus. Often assumed to be urine, it is, in fact, only water that the frog absorbs from its water dish in order to keep moist and to provide it with a store of water in case of drought.

Feeding

Australian Green Tree Frogs generally feed on insects, locusts, and earthworms, but they are also capable of eating vertebrates, such as small frogs and lizards. The occasional pinkie mouse may be offered. Only feed as much as will be consumed over a short period a few times a week. Easy to feed, these frogs enjoy food, but they are prone to obesity, so be careful not to overfeed them.

Breeding

After a resting, dry season in the wild, Australian Green Tree Frogs will usually feed, and then, stimulated by the rainfall during the beginning of the onset of the rainy season, they will breed in a few inches of water at around 77–86°F (25–30°C). Sometimes this process occurs easily, but an increase in humidity coupled with simulated rainfall may precipitate the spawning.

Between 200 and 2,000 eggs may be laid, and they will hatch within a day or so. If they are fed well on algae and other microscopic particulate foods, these tadpoles will be ready within four to six weeks to metamorphose into tiny froglets.

must know

At all stages of breeding and rearing, you must ensure that access from the water is possible— to prevent the drowning of adults or froglets. Young frogs need small vitamin supplemented foods and they will mature at around 18-24 months of age.

These frogs may change color according to the temperature within the vivarium. Individuals of the same size may easily be kept together.

American Green Tree Frog *Hyla cinerea*

Found in the forests and meadows of southern North America, these agile, slender green tree frogs have a distinct creamy white stripe extending from below the eye to the belly. Actively hunting and climbing grasses and bushes, this small 1^1/$_2$-2-inch (4-6-cm.) frog is a very visible, attractive vivarium pet.

must know

Most amphibians hibernate to avoid lethally cold winters. Emerging in spring, most species will be eager to breed. In captivity, we replicate this cooling period by gradually reducing the feeding of frogs and their temperature to 41-50°F (5-10°C). A few weeks at reduced temperatures will encourage your pets to breed once they are warmed up again. Before trying this for yourself, ask a specialist for more advice.

Creating the right environment

A semimoist vivarium suits these tree frogs. Height is essential, and several frogs may be housed in a 24 x 18 x 12-inch (60 x 46 x 30-cm.) vivarium. During the spring and summer months, a daytime temperature of 65-77°F (18-25°C) is preferred, but this can fall to as low as 54-65°F (12-18°C) at night.

A substrate of wood chips, moss, and leaves is superb, and a water dish should be available at all times. Branches or logs will offer opportunities for climbing. Robust plants, such as Philodendron, are also excellent, but artificial plants are also attractive and much easier to maintain in the vivarium.

Avoid using any unprotected lamps or bulbs because leaping frogs can be burned; fortunately, many vivaria, such as the Exo-Terra range, have mesh screens to prevent such injuries. Heater pads are fine, and full spectrum lighting is excellent.

Handling

American Green Tree Frogs are easy to handle, but ensure that your hands are wet—and also remember that the frogs may leap at a moment's notice. These creatures tame relatively quickly and they respond well to hand feeding.

Breeding

These frogs are most likely to breed after a period of winter hibernation, followed by rehousing in larger, wetter surroundings. Their short breeding season occurs around April to May, when the males call loudly for mates. After amplexus (the mating embrace), the coupling pair enter the water. Eggs are fertilized by the male as they leave the female's body, and clumps of 100–400 eggs are deposited among the water plants. Transfer these to shallow rearing containers where water is filtered, aerated and kept at around 68°F (20°C). Several days later, the larvae, or tadpoles, hatch and should be fed on microscopic organisms and fine powdered fish flakes. Metamorphosis takes about a month when the brown and green colored froglets, measuring 1/2–1 inches (1–2 cm.), are ready for a terrestrial life. These froglets mature at two to three years of age.

Although they are particularly fond of flying insects, Green Tree Frogs will just as happily eat small to medium-size crickets.

Red-Eyed Tree Frog *Agalychnis callidryas*

This is among the most stunning and desirable of the tree frogs, with blood red eyes, orange feet, and blue-and-cream flashes on its sides—observed only when the frogs are on the move. These placid and delicate frogs are frequently bred and kept in captivity.

must know

Tree frogs have evolved remarkable disklike suckers or pads at the end of each toe, giving them the ability to climb high up into bushes and trees and adhere firmly when jumping after prey or from branch to branch. Microscopic research has shown that the pads are coated with a thin mucus that adheres by wet adhesion, like wet tissue paper on glass.

Creating the right environment

Tall vivaria, measuring 18 x 24 x 12 inchs (45 x 60 x 30 cm.), furnished with mosses, real plants, and branches, provides an excellent home for these frogs, although many breeders maintain them in a more simple, laboratory-style setup. Attaining the correct balance of humidity, temperature ,and ventilation is important; they prefer 50–80 percent humidity, and a daytime temperature of 77–86°F (25–30°C), dropping to approximately 68°F (20°C) at nigh, when they become active. A water bowl must be available at all times and should be cleaned every other day because these and other amphibians absorb water into the bladder—dirty water may

One of the most attractive frogs that are available to pet keepers, the Red-Eyed Tree Frog is suitable for the more experienced keeper.

often lead to fatal infections. A ful- spectrum light source benefits most species and encourages good plant growth for naturalistic vivaria.

Handling

These bright green tree frogs are slow moving and ponderous by nature. They are nocturnal, and when they are at rest during the day their bright colors are completely concealed from view as their feet are tucked into the body and their eyes are closed; they look just like one of the leaves they prefer to rest on. Handle them cautiously, and only when necessary, because their skin is extremely delicate; it is far better to enjoy them visually. If you need to move them, wait until they are at rest on a leaf, then cut it off and place it in a small container with some air holes—keep moist and warm.

Feeding

Red-Eyed Tree Frogs prefer flying foods, such as flies and moths, but crickets and other live foods of suitable size can also be offered. Dust the foods with multivitamins and feed as much as will be eaten two to three times a week. Some extras can be left in the vivarium to be hunted later.

Breeding

In the wild, these frogs breed in bushes, shrubs, and trees that overhang water. Eggs are laid in a frothy mass on leaves, and the tadpoles, on feeling rain, drop from the leaf into the puddles below. To trigger breeding in captivity, try the simulation technique used for the Australian Tree Frogs (see page 65) but with leafy branches for them to climb on.

Growing to only 3 inches (8 cm.), this delicate, beautiful frog is best left in the vivarium and handled carefully only when necessary.

want to know more?

• There are many resources to help you to discover more about frogs. Use the Internet as a research tool or visit a library for books relating to amphibians.
• Joining a local wildlife group will help you to find out about native species in your area.
• Or visit the Amphibian Conservation web site at www.frogs.org.
• Or try herpetological societies, such as www.international-herpetological-society.org

Red-Eyed Tree Frog | 69

3 Reptiles: Lizards and tortoises

Reptiles, including lizards and tortoises, are becoming an increasingly popular choice of pet. From the incredible, color-changing Chameleon to the endearing Leopard Gecko, these creatures are surprisingly easy to look after. Most lizards are low maintenance, requiring only the occasional feeding and cleaning, and none require walks, annual injections, or grooming, but tortoises are more demanding. Other benefits are that lizards and tortoises do not affect asthmatics, make little or no noise, and can be kept in a limited space. Moreover, the vivarium your reptile lives in can be decorated like a miniature landscape, adding an attractive feature to your home.

What are reptiles?

Unlike mammals, which utilize food to maintain a steady internal temperature, the temperature of a reptile is dependent on its external environment. Reptiles are often misleadingly referred to as "cold-blooded" animals, and, during basking, their blood may reach temperatures that are warmer than that of a human.

must know

Lizards and snakes are in the order *Squamata*, with lizards split away into the suborder *Sauria*. Lizards usually possess four legs, a long tail, and moving eyelids, while snakes are limbless and have fused eyelids. Tortoises are in the order *Chelonia*. Their bony shell made of horny plates encloses a soft body; terrestrial and aquatic forms exist and there are approximately 230 species in total.

Lizards and tortoises

Lizards and tortoises are reptiles, and they need to bask in the sun or sit upon warm ground when they are cold; conversely, they must retreat into shaded areas if they are to avoid fatal overheating. Their ability to lighten or darken the skin also helps this process—lighter skin reflects heat, whereas darker skin absorbs it.

Reptile skin is effectively watertight because it is covered by protective scales. In some species, such as the tortoise, these scales are enlarged and contain bony plates, which, along with flattened and fused vertebrae, form the shell. The skin of reptiles may appear shiny but is never slimy, and after shedding is usually eaten. All lizards are vertebrate animals with an internal skeleton, from the brain-protecting skull right down through the spine, ribs, and tailbones to the (apart from legless species) tiny leg and toe bones.

Species of lizards

Over 3,500 species of lizard are known and, although they are bound by common characteristics, there is considerable variation in their diet, habitat, and behavior. Most species are predators, eating rodents,

There are at least 3,500 species of lizard discovered so far, of which only a few are suitable as pets. Herpetology is the study of both reptiles and amphibians.

amphibians, and insects, but some consume both plant and animal matter (omnivores), and a few are entirely herbivorous, existing on fruit, flowers, and leaves. Many are solitary by nature, congregating only to breed, although some exhibit complex family or group dynamics.

Egg layers

The majority of lizards and all chelonia (tortoises and turtles) are egg layers. Eggs may be deposited into leaf litter, buried in a hole dug in the ground or even stuck to tree bark or vegetation. Some eggs have a hard shell, whereas others have a leathery, parchmentlike texture. Once eggs are laid, they are incubated by environmental warmth alone. Reptile young are always born, or hatch, as miniature replicas of their parents—no metamorphic stage exists as it does in amphibians.

This tortoise is one of a huge number of reptiles now bred in captivity as pets, ensuring that high-quality animals are available without affecting wild populations.

Leopard Gecko *Eublepharis macularius*

Unlike most members of the *Gekkonidae* family, these striking and attractive geckos are not noted for their climbing abilities because they lack "adhesive" pads on their digits. They are ground dwelling and have small sharp claws.

An excellent introduction to reptile keeping, this attractive lizard is a popular choice for the inexperienced pet keeper.

Natural habitat

Spotted like the big cat that shares their name, these geckos are terrestrial and adapted to life in the harsh, arid rocky deserts of northwestern India, Pakistan, Iran, and Iraq. Living alone or in small groups, they avoid the fatally hot daytime by hiding under rocks and boulders. The fully grown adults measure around 8 inches (20–22cm) in length, and these pretty yellow-and-mauve reptiles can live for up to 30 years as pets.

Creating the right environment

Ideally, your Leopard Gecko should be housed separately, where there is no competition for food or for shelters. A 24 x 12 x 12-inch (60 x 30 x 30-cm.) vivarium will provide ample space for a single specimen. Larger vivaria, such as 36 x 24 x 12 inches (90 x 60 x 30 cm.), would be suitable for a trio of geckos—all females or two females and one male—and gives you the creative opportunity to make an attractive desertlike setup for your pets.

If a temperature range of 80–88°F (27–32°C) is maintained and your setup provides the essentials of food, water, and shelter, your gecko should thrive. A heater pad is all that is required to ensure adequate warmth. By placing it at one end of the vivarium,

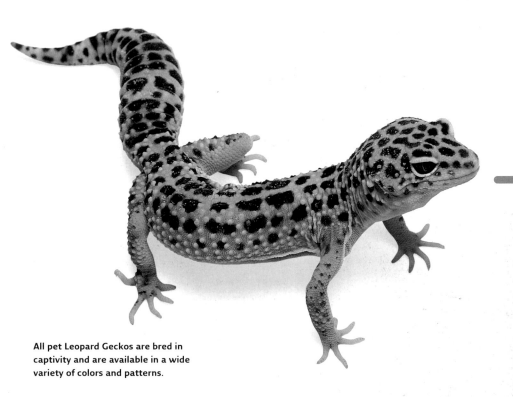

All pet Leopard Geckos are bred in captivity and are available in a wide variety of colors and patterns.

your pet can warm up or cool down (thermoregulate) as it wants. Coir chippings, pea gravel, and wood chips—or just some paper—can be used as a base or substrate. Live succulents and other "house" plants can be added to create a decorative effect. Simply bury the pot in some substrate away from the heat source and don't forget to water the plant. A piece of driftwood is also highly effective and will give your gecko something to climb on.

Clean creatures

Geckos are clean creatures and will select and use a toilet site. Their droppings dry quickly, and they should be removed on a regular basis. Even in groups, most vivaria will require a complete clean out only once every few months.

must know

Most reptiles benefit greatly from the addition of a humidity chamber somewhere in the vivarium. A pile of plastic plants or some real moss, regularly mist sprayed and enclosed in a box that your lizard can enter at will, is useful for preventing dehydration and helps to facilitate periodic skin shedding.

Feeding

Leopard Geckos should be fed every other day or so. They can consume most small to medium live foods, such as crickets, a few of which should be placed within the vivarium for your lizard to stalk as desired. Being nocturnal, most feeding will occur overnight. Water, replaced regularly, should always be available in a shallow dish on the ground, and occasional mist spraying is enjoyed and beneficial.

Handling

Leopard Geckos tolerate handling well, although it is best to sit down when handling any reptile in case it is dropped or jumps out of your hand. The best time to start taming your lizard is while it is still young. Handle it for short, regular periods to show your pet you pose no threat to its safety.

Handling from an early age will ensure your Leopard Gecko grows into a tame and friendly adult.

Breeding

Leopard Geckos breed well in captivity. Mating usually occurs unseen in a covered area, and the first signs of a successful coupling is the female's noticeably swollen belly. Each female can lay several clutches of two eggs per year. Try to encourage her to lay her eggs in a suitable spot—an upturned plastic container, with a hole cut in one side and filled with moistened vermiculite, is ideal.

The two eggs, being a standard clutch for most geckos, should be transferred to an incubator to prevent desiccation. Unlike many bird eggs, reptile eggs should not be turned—simply place them in the incubating medium and cover. Provide airflow but keep humidity at 70-80 percent and maintain a temperature of 86°F (30°C).

The incubating eggs should be checked on a regular basis—very shrivelled or moldy ones should be removed to avoid contaminating healthy eggs. A white but slightly indented egg needs a higher humidity level. The young will hatch after 6 to 12 weeks. The juveniles are marked with yellow-and-black bands that will gradually break up into the familiar adult markings. They should be housed in small rearing containers, separately if possible. If kept communally, you must provide several hiding places and water dishes, removing the more dominant individuals once they begin to harass others. A daily misting will ensure good skin condition and ease frequent shedding as the juveniles grow. Small crickets and waxworms are ideal first foods—geckos also adore small spiders. All foodstuffs should be lightly dusted with a multivitamin and mineral supplement.

must know

A Leopard Gecko sheds, or sloughs, its skin on a regular basis as it grows. The peeling skin is fine and translucent and the lizards normally eat it. Probably nutritious, and, by eating it, predators are less likely to detect a gecko's presence. Your lizard fades in color as the shedding begins. A new more colorful skin is revealed as the old one is consumed. Some species, such as Blue-Tongued Skinks, simply leave the skin behind and wander off.

Peacock Day Gecko *Phelsuma quadriocellata*

Delightful little jewels, Peacock Day Geckos can make a vivarium come alive with flashes of color as they patrol their territory. Compared to other Day Geckos, this spotted variety is a dwarf species reaching only 3 inches (7.5 cm.) in length.

must know

Whereas most geckos are nocturnal and somewhat dull in color, Day Geckos are active by day and the most flamboyant members of the *Gekkonidae* family. Day geckos have no movable eyelids and use their tongue to wipe clean and moisturize their eyes.

Habitat and appearance

Day Geckos are found on islands in the Indian Ocean: Madagascar, Mauritius, and the Seychelles. The Peacock Day Gecko has a peacocklike eye marking on either side of the body behind the front legs, red spots and blobs on the back, and a vivid "V" on its face.

Creating the right environment

A 20 x 12 x 24-inch (50 x 30 x 60 cm.) vivarium is really suitable for only a single lizard. Males should be housed either individually or one male with several females. With larger vivaria, it is much easier to create a suitable environment for a harem of lizards to enjoy—without adequate space, food, or basking opportunity, some individuals could be bullied. A maximum temperature of 88°F (32°C) should be maintained during the day, which can fall at night to a cooler 68–72°F (20–22°C).

Handling

Day Geckos are virtually impossible to hold, so enjoy these creatures bounding around their vivarium. If you need to transport or move one, place a clear plastic container over the lizard and slide a piece of thin cardboard underneath to contain it.

Feeding

Day Geckos are small arboreal lizards and only little foods are suitable—small crickets, waxmoth larvae, and flies are relished. Live foods can be dusted with vitamin and mineral supplements as recommended. While essentially insectivores, their habit of licking fruit is well known, and small chunks of sweet fruit, such as mango or grape, and honey or jam are enjoyed. Mist spraying morning and night should keep humidity levels high in glass vivaria.

Breeding

Once Day Geckos are settled in a vivarium, breeding is sure to follow. Day Geckos, unlike most other reptiles, lay hard calciferous eggs, which in most cases adhere to almost any surface, from the glass or wooden side of the vivarium to a bamboo pole. Don't try to cut or remove them, but ensure that the eggs are warmed sufficiently to incubate successfully just where they are.

Standing's Day Gecko *Phelsuma standingi*

These Day Geckos grow up to 10 inches (25 cm.) in length and can live for up to 10 years in captivity. Native to a restricted area in parts of southwestern Madagascar, they inhabit more arid, thorny forests than the lush, densely planted areas favored by most Day Geckos.

must know

The only home for Standings Gecko may soon be in captivity because their natural habitat is disappearing fast. Forests and scrubland are cleared for agriculture and other developments that benefit mankind, and over 75 percent of Madagascar's natural forests are long gone already. By keeping and learning about these lizards, we may help a species that is sadly likely to disappear in the wild.

Creating the right environment

Like all Day Geckos, little time is spent on the ground, so you can dispense with ground coverings or substrate. You can line the cage with newspaper for ease of cleaning, but large pebbles or natural decor, such as bamboo, are more attractive. A pair or trio (one male and two females) can be housed in a 24 x 24 x 24-inch (60 x 60 x 60 cm.) vivarium. While mist spraying is needed for drinking, this species seems to prefer slightly higher, more steady temperatures of about 88°F (32°C) and lower humidity (70-75 percent) than other Day Geckos. At night, as temperatures drop to 65-72°F (18-22°C), they will sleep on leaves or in a sheltered piece of tree bark.

Handling

Day Geckos are not an easily handled species and are best kept to observe and enjoy as the colorful creatures they are. For advice on transporting or moving a Day Gecko, see page 79.

Feeding

Large Day Geckos can eat most insects available to the enthusiast. Beetle grubs and crickets are relished, and most foodstuffs should be regularly dusted with vitamin/mineral supplements to ensure optimum health. Sweet fruit and nectar are best offered high up in the vivarium on tiny bottle tops or upturned jar lids. Food can be offered at feeding stations by placing insects in suspended plastic pet homes that the lizard can reach at will, but from which the insects cannot escape. "Take-out" food insects will need pieces of orange or apple to ensure that they, too, can eat and drink. For water, mist spray, but this gecko will learn to drink from a shallow dish placed high within the vivarium instead of at ground level.

Breeding

Females, upon maturing, are easily sexed by the calcium deposit bulges on their necks, which can grow alarmingly large but are entirely natural. Males have a more slender neck and frame and "V"-shaped indented preanal pores on their undersides. Eggs hatch after 50–60 days, sticking together in one or two batches in the vivarium on glass or bamboo. A pair may produce eggs for around six months of the year but need to be well fed with nourishing food to sustain this rate of production. Females will not only guard their eggs but also protect baby Day Geckos for several months after hatching.

Although patterns and colors vary in this species, these geckos tend to have sky blue skin and green heads with black, crazy-paving, netlike patterns.

Giant Day Gecko *Phelsuma madagascarensis*

These stunning lizards are easy to keep and breed. Their skin is an electric lime green and they can have, depending on the exact subspecies, orange-red markings in the form of dots or blobs along the back and between the nostrils and eyes. Active by day, these large geckos can reach 10 inches (25 cm.) in length.

must know

Day Geckos are fond of sweet fruit and plant saps. A halved grape, positioned securely high in the vivarium, will attract a gecko for a prolonged licking session. Licking foods no doubt provide essential minerals and vitamins for these sweet-toothed lizards.

The tiny suction pads on geckos' toes enable them to grip and climb even the smoothest surface.

Creating the right environment

A planted vivarium will make the most attractive display for these pretty geckos. A huge range of house plants available from garden centers are suitable, but among the easiest to maintain are philodendrons, ficus, yuccas, hoya, oleander, and passionflower. The use of full-spectrum lamps will assist both your plants and your lizards in growing and developing naturally. However, you must ensure that growing plants do not interfere with the heating or lighting equipment. Artificial plants are just as effective and come without any maintenance issues, apart from washing.

In the vivarium, replicate a tropical temperature range of 77–88°F (25–32°C). These lizards enjoy humidity levels reaching 80 percent, so mist spray or add a reptile water feature. Fresh air is greatly appreciated and you should always keep your vivarium well ventilated.

It is best to keep these territorial geckos singly or as one male to two or more females if space is available. A 24 x 24 x 24-inch (60 x 60 x 60-cm.) vivarium is ample for two to three individuals, while 24 x 18 x 12 inches (60 x 45 x 30 cm.) is fine for a single gecko; the bigger and taller the vivarium the better.

Handling

You are unlikely to ever handle a Giant Day Gecko. If they are physically restrained, you will risk tearing their delicate skin and they are far too active to sit still on you.

Feeding

The majority of food eaten by these lizards is insect matter, and both crawling and flying foods are taken with gusto. They love to drink from droplets, so spray regularly to ensure that they do not get thirsty. They will soon learn to use a water feature.

Breeding

If geckoes are kept in adult groups, breeding is likely. Look out for the typical clutch of two hard-shelled eggs of $1/2$ inch (1 cm.) across. Leave in the vivarium to hatch—hopefully, the female will have deposited them where the temperatures of 77–86°F (25–30°C) will incubate them in around 45–60 days.

must know

These agile lizards have adapted to an arboreal lifestyle. The suction pads on each digit ensure they get a good grip on shiny, slippery leaves—even the sides of a vivarium or glass— as well as the rough bark on trees and palms. Each toe is covered on the underside with fine hairlike structures that grip to most surfaces. Many geckos can run across, and even live on, the ceiling of a room.

This muscular lizard looks in excellent health. Day Geckos do not have movable eyelids and keep their large eyes clean with regular licks from the tongue.

Green Anole *Anolis carolinensis*

Anoles are charming small lizards and a popular choice of pet. They leap and dart about, providing you with hours of visual entertainment. Active during daylight hours, the males are highly territorial and aggressive to one another, signaling with bright flashes of color from their throat fans, or dewlaps.

must know

Sometimes called American Chameleons, Anoles are native to the southern United States, Central America, and the Caribbean, where they can be found on walls, fences, and shrubs in yards and other man-made settlements. Green Anoles measure 5-8 inches (13-20 cm.) in length and can live for three to five years.

Creating the right environment

Anoles will thrive in a tall vivarium with either real or replica plants and branches. A harem of four females to one male is about the best ratio for a community setup in a vivarium measuring at least 36 x 24 x 12 inches (90 x 60 x 30 cm.). You can minimize competition for the best basking spot by offering two or more options. A temperature range of 75-86°F (24-30°C) is ideal, and ful-spectrum lighting will assist both the healthy development of lizards and plants. Nighttime temperatures can safely drop to 68°F (20°C).

This species really appreciates humidity as well as fresh air. Regular mist spraying will assist, but adding a water feature, dripper, or mister will help raise humidity levels generally.

Handling

Although fast and able to leap about, an Anole will learn to sit on your hand in exchange for a tasty treat. These small and delicate lizards need a gentle touch, and allowing one to climb onto your hand is less stressful for the animal. If you want to move your pet, grip it firmly but gently. This is a lizard that is much better for observing than handling.

Feeding

These insectivores will eat any small to medium live insect foods. Mealworms should be avoided because many will pass through them undigested. Feed at least twice weekly, watching to ensure that every occupant gets several insects per feeding. A small surplus amount of live food may be present in the vivarium at all times. Mist spraying once a day or so is essential, because Anoles prefer to drink water droplets from leaves instead of still water from a bowl. Or consider a drip system or mister.

Breeding

Once you establish a group of these lizards and they are well fed and happy, breeding is sure to follow. One or two eggs are laid about two weeks after mating. These will be buried by the female, pushed by her nose into the compost in a warm and damp area, frequently either around the pot or roots of a climbing plant, such as Philodendron. The tiny baby Anoles will need equally tiny fruit flies and micro crickets to start feeding on.

Adult male Anoles are more brightly colored than females, and only males display using their colorful throat fans, or dewlaps, accompanied by head bobbing.

Blue-Tongued Skink *Tiliqua sp.*

Skinks are a widespread family of lizards found around the globe in both temperate and tropical areas. More than 1,200 species are known to science, but few are as attractive or as easy to keep or breed as the magnificent Blue-Tongue.

must know

As the name suggests, these lizards have a lovely big blue tongue. If threatened, this can be flattened and rippled inside an open mouth which, accompanied by a hiss, acts as an effective deterrent to would-be predators.

Appearance and habitat

These stocky 20-inch (50-cm.) lizards have overlapping scales and can be found on the ground in Australia and Tasmania, where they live among leaf litter, consuming invertebrates and snails as well as fruit—many live underground. New species of skink are still being discovered, but they all have certain characteristics in common. Skinks are noted for their long flattened, shiny bodies and degenerate or reduced limbs—some are completely limbless, while other types have very small and weak legs.

Most skinks are omnivorous and, including the Blue-tongue, give birth to live young, instead of laying eggs. They may live for 10–15 years. Juvenile skinks are particularly vulnerable to introduced predators, such as cats in Australia, and are diminishing in numbers right across their range.

Creating the right environment

Blue-Tongued Skinks should be kept singly as a rule because they can be aggressive toward one another. A dry, woodland type of habitat is ideal for this totally terrestrial species. The ground can be covered in cork logs for retreats and decorated for visual effect with leaf litter, twigs, and mossy rocks. Remember that these lizards root around under ground debris looking for food, so, therefore, a delicately planted vivarium would be quickly ruined.

A vivarium for a single skink should measure at least 48 x 12 x 12 inches (120 x 30 x 30 cm) with a daytime temperature gradient of 77-95°F (25-35°C), falling at night to 65-68°F (18-20°C). The combination of a heater pad at one end and a thermostatically controlled spotlight, wired up to a timer switch, will warm the tank and create a daytime basking area. Timing the light to switch off during the evening will automatically reduce the temperature. Full-spectrum lighting is generally recommended for successful long-term care and breeding, but any exposure to natural sunlight outside is a good thing. Many people keep this species in outdoor enclosures when it is warm enough, but ensure they cannot escape and are safe from predators.

Young captive bred Blue-Tongues are normally acquired when they are about a couple of months old. With regular handling, they can become very tame.

Handling

The temperament of lizards can vary, just like people, but for many years the Blue-Tongue Lizard has been considered a good choice for close contact. They are normally tolerant of handling and enjoy a stroke or scratch. Their small claws may feel sharp on younger hands and they always need to feel supported under their body and legs.

Feeding

My Blue-Tongued Skinks enjoy variations of the diet that is described below, but they can easily become obese, so be careful not to feed them every day.

must know

The skin of lizards varies greatly but is based upon the "scale" in all species. Blue-Tongued Skinks have tough, almost armored, scales for rummaging in the Australian bush. Scales are made of keratin, a fibrous structural protein, which is also a component of nails, hair, horns, and feathers.

These scavenging omnivores enjoy a huge range of vegetables, fruit, and flowers.

A large batch of food can be prepared at one time and then frozen in small portions for later use. Mango, apple, banana, berries, salad greens, and peas, for example, can be finely chopped and then mixed with a little dog food or ground beef, much to the lizard's satisfaction. Snails are also relished, with the shell being crunched and then spat out. A good balance to aim for is roughly 70 percent greens and fruit to 30 percent meat.

Offer your pet fresh food three or four times a week in a shallow dish; uneaten foods should be removed within a few hours. Pinkies are also easy and nutritious foods. Water should be available to drink and these lizards will love a mist spray. The moist conditions will stimulate them to emerge and look for their food. They are particularly keen to feed after shedding their skin.

Popular medium-size lizards, these impressive skinks are easy to maintain and enjoy a variety of readily available foodstuffs.

Breeding

Producing between 6 and 20 live young once a year, Blue-Tongue Skinks can be a prolific species. Breeding is possible at two to three years with adult lizards, introduced in spring after a cooling-off period. Males grab and bite females around the neck before mating takes place.

Sexing

When mating is observed, this is probably the only time you can reliably tell the male from the female. Sexing is not easy but females will tend to have a broader body, while males may just show signs of penile bulges at the base of the tail when viewed from underneath. These are live-bearing lizards and worth the effort to breed.

Bearded Dragon *Pogona vitticeps*

A remarkable Australian native, the Bearded Dragon is noted for its ease of care and good temperament, living to around ten years old. In the wild, these Dragon lizards are equally at home in lush suburban yards or the more open and hot desert.

Dragon lizards are dramatic and active vivarium pets.

Appearance

Diurnal and 16–24 inches (40–60 cm.) in length, this is a medium-size but heavy-bodied, omnivorous reptile. The name in part comes from their extendible beard. The back, head, and tail are rough to the touch, while the belly is white and soft. Along both sides of the body runs a line of fine long spines, which help camouflage the lizard by breaking up its visible outline when it presses against the branch of a tree.

Creating the right environment

A dry woodland or desert-style vivarium is suitable for these lizards. A unit measuring 36 x 20 x 36 inches (90 x 50 x 90 cm.) is suitable for an adult pair or trio (two females and one male). Two young Beardies would need at least a 24 x 12 x 12-inch (60 x 30 x 30-cm.) vivarium for the first few months of their life. Unless you intend to breed them, it is best to house and keep them alone, or to keep only females together because males become territorial.

Provide cork logs or rocks for climbing on or burrowing under, and cover the vivarium floor with bark chips or play sand. If two or more Beardies are kept together, several basking areas must be provided to minimize competition. Temperatures can reach as high as 104°F (40°C) at the basking end of their setup, but can be reduced to 68°F (20°C) at night. Heater pads are useful to ensure that an area of substrate is warm and dry at all times, and full-spectrum lighting is essential for healthy growth and development.

A clean shallow dish of fresh water should always be available for drinking, and your Bearded Dragon will enjoy an occasional mist spraying or supervised bath. Soiled areas need regular cleaning.

Handling

These lizards become tame quickly while they are still young. Regular handling at this stage should ensure that your lizard remains willing to be handled. They are unlikely to ever try to bite you. If unwilling to be picked up, they will usually just walk or jump away.

Feeding

These are omnivorous lizards with a good appetite; they are prone, if anything, to overeating. A well-supplemented diet is recommended, especially for

Young Bearded Dragon lizards become tame easily when frequently handled by keepers.

the fast-growing juveniles. A vast range of food types may be offered, including commercially farmed insects, some processed dried lizard foods, and pinkies for their nutritional value. Plant material, such as collard greens and dandelion flowers and leaves, are relished and should be chopped for smaller individuals to manage easily. A well-defined social hierarchy develops within any group of Bearded Dragons, and at feeding time it is interesting to observe their behavior. The largest or most dominant lizard will feed first, the others waiting and watching with their tails clearly bent upward, signaling their lowly status.

Only after the dominant lizard has finished his meal and moves away do the other subordinate lizards get their chance to feed. If keeping a group of Dragon lizards, it is essential to provide ample basking sites and adequate food, so that all the members of your family group can thrive.

An adult Bearded Dragon in relaxed pose. When threatened, it will puff up its spiky beard from which it derives its name.

Breeding

Bearded Dragons become sexually mature between their first and second years. Both sexes have spines on the head, neck, and throat, but only males develop the coal-black throat and tail tip during courtship, or when involved in ritualistic fighting over territory. This will be accompanied by much head-bobbing.

A healthy female may lay six clutches of eggs in a season, averaging 20 eggs per clutch. These are buried deep into the soil—up to 8 inches (20 cm.)—or into a laying box containing vermiculite. They need to be incubated at 84°F (29°C) for about 60 days. After producing eggs or live young, herptiles benefit from a period of isolation and a nutrition-packed diet in order to recover for future breeding.

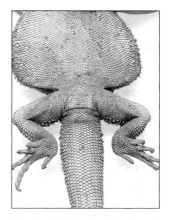

Females either lack or have much less prominent pores around the thighs or anal area.

Sexing a lizard

Lizards usually have visual characteristics that make it easy to sex them. Most lizards can be easily sexed by the time they are one year old. It helps to have several individuals of the same age to compare the differences. The following guidelines should help.

1 Most, but not all, male lizards are larger and stronger looking than females.

2 Males usually have thicker and longer tails than female lizards.

Males usually have thicker and longer tails than females and more noticeable pores. Maturing male beardies are easily sexed by their extendible black beard.

3 Males have larger more colorful dewlaps, bigger head crests, and even horns.

4 Females lack entirely or have less prominent pores around the cloacal area or on the thighs. To examine these, hold the lizard firmly and then turn it upside down. They look just like ordinary scales but are often marked with a dimple and clearly visible in a "V" shape just above the anal opening.

Veiled Chameleon *Chameleo calyptratus*

Chameleons are unlike any other lizards and are a favorite choice for anyone who is interested in fantastic reptiles. Also called the Yemen Chameleon, this lizard is native to Saudi Arabia and Yemen.

must know

This species is captive bred in large numbers and would appear to be one of the most adaptable chameleon species for the pet keeper willing to invest some time and effort. With a two-to-eight-year life span, these are short-lived lizards. Males grow to 24 inches (60 cm.), females up to 13 inches (33 cm.).

Creating the right environment

Like many lizards, chameleons like furnishings in the vivarium to remain in the same place, so place plants, branches, or watering areas in permanent sites. Chameleons are best housed in larger vivaria: a single specimen needs a 36 x 36 x 20-inch (90 x 90 x 50-cm.) vivarium and a daytime temperature of 68–86°F (20–30°C). Like most lizards, the males are solitary and aggressive, so they are best kept singly.

As chameleons are bush or shrub dwellers, offer living plants or, at least, sturdy plastic plants and branches on which to climb. Position spotlights that create basking areas away from live or plastic plants because they may singe or melt. Full-spectrum lighting will ensure good plant and pet growth. Mist spray daily and/or provide a circulating water feature to keep humidity levels up. Make sure there is good ventilation without causing chilly drafts.

Handling

Most Veiled Chameleons tolerate handling relatively well, especially if it involves hand feeding. Start while your pet is young to condition it to this type of contact on a regular basis. Never pick up the chameleon because this causes great offense and visible stress. Instead, let it climb up onto your hand and fingers or a small handheld branch.

Feeding

Chameleons need to eat and
drink regularly, with water being
preferred in droplet form. All live foods can be
tried, but climbing or flying insects are best. Vary
the diet to provide a range of vitamins and minerals.
Some yard-caught food is advised, and larger Veiled
Chameleons may accept highly nutritious pinkies.
This lizard will also eat a range of leaves, fruit, and
vegetables. These and, indeed, all foods should be
dusted with vitamin and mineral supplements.

The fascinating Veiled Chameleon
is easy to keep and the most
commonly bred chameleon species.

Breeding

These lizards are prolific egg layers, and a female
may lay clutches numbering between 25 and
80 eggs, three to four times a year. This productivity
does take its toll eventually and females rarely
survive much beyond their fifth clutch. The eggs
are buried in soil or sand and should be placed in
vermiculite and incubated at 80–85°F (27–29.5°C)
during the day, with a small nighttime drop in
temperature to 75°F (24°C). Juvenile chameleons
grow rapidly and it is in these first crucial months
that a varied and well-supplemented diet will
enable them to grow up into healthy, mature
specimens. They need a larger range and variety
of insect prey than the adults, which tend to enjoy
a more omnivorous diet. Growing fast, they need
to be separated within 10–12 weeks.

Panther Chameleon

Chameleo pardalis (now officially Furcifer pardalis)

These large colorful lizards are well worth the extra care that is required to ensure success within the vivarium. Native to Madagascar, they can also be found on a few neighboring islands, such as Mauritus and Reunion, where they have been introduced to control pest insects on plantations.

must know

Entirely diurnal, these short-lived creatures have a lifespan of about two to three years, and they range in size from 13 inches (33 cm.) for females to 20 inches (51 cm.) for males.

Appearance

Probably the most incredible lizards of all, chameleons are a true wonder of the natural world. They are noted for their many unusual features: they have amazing color changing abilities, independently moving eyes, and an incredible, extendible tongue. The chameleon's amazing ability to change color is much misunderstood. Emotions and territorial posturing, as well as camouflage, are responsible for the array of colors exhibited. Chameleons are very desirable as pets.

Creating the right environment

Unless a large enclosure is available for a pair or trio (two females to one male), Panther Chameleons are best kept singly. Males are territorial and will fight and injure one another if kept together, but if housed alone they appear to be easier to keep and are of less nervous disposition than the females. I would recommend a minimum 24 x 24 x 24-inch (60 x 60 x 60-cm.) vivarium for juveniles or solitary individuals, but the optimum size would be 24 x 72 x 24 inches (60 x 180 x 60 cm.), the greater height adds more scope to create an attractive setup.

A temperature gradient of 78-95°F (26-35°C) is ideal, and full-spectrum lighting is essential unless regular exposure to natural sunlight is available. Panther Chameleons cannot tolerate temperatures lower than 68°F (20°C) and must always be warm. Do remember, however, never to place your vivarium near a window to provide extra sunshine for your pet. The useful ultraviolet rays will not penetrate glass or plastic anyway and may turn your vivarium into an oven with direct sunlight lifting the temperature to a fatally high level.

One or more spotlights are best used to create a basking area, and you may consider ceramic heaters for cooler nights. Provide branches and plants, real or plastic, for your pet to climb on but try to keep them in the same places—lizards like familiarity.

Humidity and ventilation

These chameleons prefer a higher humidity for at least part of the day—around 75 percent. They also prefer to drink from droplets on leaves. Compared to other lizards, they do tend to drink a lot of water and inhabit areas in the wild with high rainfall and moisture. Conditions must not get stale within the vivarium, so good ventilation and fresh air are key. A small fan can help circulate and freshen the air but it must always be placed out of reach of the vivarium's inhabitants.

Male Panther Chameleons are more colorful than the females, and may be green, red, orange, lemon, or even turquoise.

The Chameleon's foot is uniquely adapted to its climbing lifestyle; as seen above, its opposing toes provide an excellent grip.

The chameleon's skin contains many chromatophores (pigment-filled cells), which enable rapid change in skin coloration.

Handling

Some chameleons will tolerate handling by their keepers relatively well, especially if it involves hand feeding. Start handling your pet when it is still young to condition it to this kind of contact on a regular basis. Never pick up a chameleon, but, instead, let it climb up onto your hand and fingers. If permitted to do so, it will continue to climb until it reaches your shoulders and head.

Feeding

Panthers are insectivorous, eating most live foods and the odd pink mouse. Flying or climbing insect prey is preferred, and variety is the key to providing vitamins and minerals for healthy development. Chameleons like, and need, a lot of food, but there is less risk of obesity with these lizards than other species. They drink more than other reptiles,

must know

The chameleon's tongue is a complex but highly effective hunting tool. It is like a long, hollow tube, along the length of which runs a powerful muscle that can be expanded or relaxed at will. Each expansion shoots the tongue out from its anchor point in the floor of the mouth. The tip of the tongue is bulbous and coated in tacky secretions designed to hold the prey firmly while the tongue recoils back into the mouth. Each eye is capable of moving independently and of judging distance. The chameleon can then "shoot" with its tongue with deadly accuracy—but don't blink; it all happens incredibly quickly.

preferring droplets to still water in a bowl. Mist spray daily and/or provide a water dripping system.

Live foods

One method of supplying live foods without insects dispersing into the vivarium is to attach an opaque pet home, or similar steep and smooth-sided bowl, to a feeding branch. This will position food within the range of the chameleon and its tongue, without enabling the bugs to reach the branch to escape. Make sure the bug home is well stocked and the bugs are well fed—the chameleon will use this station for the occasional snack.

Breeding

About a month after a successful mating, the female will lay 20-30 eggs, which are typically chameleon: white, oval, and parchmentlike in appearance. These will be buried in the egg-laying material that should already have been provided. The eggs need to be incubated in vermiculite, and from start to finish hatching of the whole batch may vary between 160 and 360 days. It is always worth having a laying box with some vermiculite available for your female chameleons. Vermiculite is a herpetologist's favorite breeding medium because it is light, sterile, and absorbs moisture readily. Sponge chips is another alternative used by some breeders.

Chameleons can climb extremely quickly when necessary, the long prehensile tail acting like a fifth limb. When they are hunting, their movements are slow and deliberate; when on the ground, they are much more cautious.

Uromastyx *Uromastyx acanthinurus*

Uromastyx, sometimes called Spiny Tailed Agamas, have a dry, parchmentlike skin. Their color varies from dull brown to sandy yellow or brick red. These inquisitive lizards make endearing pets with their tortoiselike head and postures. They are friendly creatures and can live for around 15 years.

must know

This tough-looking lizard thrives in the harsh, hot desertlike conditions found in the southern Mediterranean and Middle East and can grow to about 18 inches (45 cm.). On cold nights, they wedge themselves between rocks.

Creating the right environment

Uromastyx are best kept individually—they are not a social species. Juveniles can be reared best in small plastic pet-home type units. Larger individuals and adults require vivaria large enough to run about in; 60 x 20 x 20 inches (120 x 50 x 50 cm.) is adequate for one lizard, but the larger the better, especially if you want to keep them in pairs or small groups.

Sturdy rocks with gravel or play sand make a good base. Provide a few retreats at the cooler end of the vivarium. In the wild, temperatures can reach over 118°C (45°C) and, to avoid overheating, Uromastyx retreat into cool burrows. Make them in a vivarium from drainpipes or cork logs, but ensure that no heavy rocks or logs can collapse and injure your pet.

These lizards need the benefit of full-spectrum light and hot basking areas, controlled by a thermostat. At the hottest point in the vivarium, temperatures should reach 95°F (35°C); the rest needs to be cooler at around 68-75°F (20-24°C). This is easier to achieve in larger vivaria. Nighttime temperatures can also drop to 75°F (24°C). You can offer water a couple of times a week in shallow, accessible dishes. Mist spray occasionally, and a monthly bath or soak in a large dish is likely to be appreciated.

Handling

Uromastyx are not nervous creatures and, with patience, especially if you're starting out with a juvenile, your lizard will come to you for food. Slow movements are less likely to startle it, and eventually it should sit on your hand, at least for a while.

Feeding

Feed mainly green leaf foods with added pieces of vegetable and fruit. Food items should be finely chopped, especially for juveniles. Some insects may be accepted—up to three to five percent of their diet. Feed every other day. Most of their water needs are met through food intake, so keep foods moist. Don't worry unduly if your pet rests without eating for one or two weeks. In the wild, this species estivates at least for short periods, spending the summer or dry conditions in a dormant state.

Breeding

Mating occurs in spring and eggs should be incubated in dryish vermiculite at 86-89°F (30-33°C) for about 12 weeks. After mating, house the female on her own with a suitable amount of substrate to encourage egg laying.

must know

These lizards can wedge themselves into crevices and puff up their bellies to make it difficult for any predators to extract them. They have a special spiky clublike tail that can inflict serious wounds on their main predator, the venomous Horned Viper.

This delightful herbivorous lizard enjoys an occasional bath or spray with tepid water. The skin darkens and the body swells as life-giving water is absorbed. They grow to about 18 inches (45 cm.).

Savannah Monitor *Varanus exanthematicus*

Savannah Monitors are mostly found in grassland habitats across a wide area of Africa. They make excellent pets and can become extremely tame and placid—in fact, so laid back that they have a tendency to slothfulness and obesity if overfed and under-exercised. Reaching 40 inches (1 m.) long, they should live 15 years in captivity.

must know

Australia is the true home of Monitors, where most of the species are found. Here, they are called "Goannas." Monitors are members of the *Varanidae* family, which number around 40 species, including the world's largest lizard, *V. komodoensis*, or the Komodo Dragon, at 10 feet (3 m.).

Behavior of Monitors

These big, powerful reptiles are the juggernauts of the lizard world, capable of digging up riverbanks and termite mounds in search of food or shelter. As hunters, they are constantly on the look out for small animal prey and will climb trees, swim rivers, and dig up other reptile eggs for a meal.

Creating the right environment

Savannah Monitors should be housed individually. A vivarium measuring 48 x 18 x 18 inches (120 x 45 x 45 cm.) is adequate. Monitors require sturdy rocks, logs, and heavy-duty water bowls. A cork or drainpipe shelter is essential in the cooler end of the vivarium. Movable furnishings, such as large pebbles, can offer temporary refuges for insects. This will encourage foraging activity as your Monitor moves the pebbles to get the tasty bugs. A simple setup is best, using a paper floor covering and a couple of main objects for basking on and hiding within. The daytime temperature gradient should range from 82–88°F (28–32°C), falling to 75°F (24°C) at night. Mist spraying biweekly should keep the humidity up at around 60 percent. Bathing is much enjoyed by Monitors, and a weekly soak ensures your pet gets enough moisture and has the option of a long drink. Many lizards are stimulated to defecate in water, so water bowls must be cleaned regularly and fresh water given when fouling is noticed.

Handling

If purchased young, these Monitors should become tame and suitable for occasional handling. They are usually placid, thriving in captivity and enjoying human companionship. I have never encountered aggression, although a bad Monitor bite would be painful and might require stitches.

Savannah Monitors are also sometimes known as Bosc Monitors. This lizard may grow up to 40 inches (1 m.) in length.

Feeding

Monitors catch and consume their food whole. Young ones can be offered pinkies and larger insects. Adults eat whole adult mice and larger insect-type foods, such as locusts and snails. Feed two to three times a week as much as will be eaten in a three-to-five-minute period. Live insects scattered in the vivarium encourages foraging.

These placid lizards have heavy "armored" scales and long sharp claws for digging and climbing.

Breeding

Few people breed Monitors in captivity, and you need a considerable amount of space. A female lizard will lay 20–50 eggs once a year. These are buried about 12 inches (30 cm.) deep and need to be incubated for four to five months at around 84–88°F (29–32°C).

Water Dragon *Physignathus concincinus*

Water Dragons are an attractive lizard, with a long row of erect dragonlike scales running along the back. Their overall color is green, but the cheeks or jowls of the more mature males are enlarged and adorned with large pink scales. This makes these placid creatures look formidable.

must know

Native to the steamy jungles of southeast Asia, Water Dragons are found in India, China, and Thailand. They display well in the vivarium and reach 30-40 inches (75-100 cm.). They can probably live for 15 years and may be kept communally in larger enclosures with Basilisks or smaller Iguanids, because these species enjoy living in very similar conditions.

Creating the right environment

Larger vivaria suit these semiarboreal lizards and a 36 x 36 x 24-inch (90 x 90 x 60-cm.) vivarium gives room for all the essentials for optimum care. Although males are less aggressive to one another than other species, only keep them alone or in the company of one or more females. Juvenile Dragons, for the first year of life, can be kept in smaller units measuring, say, 36 x 12 x 18 inches (90 x 30 x 45 cm.).

These reptiles prefer semi-moist tropical conditions with a temperature range of 77–82°F (25–28°C), achievable with heater pads and spotlights, which may reduce at night to 68–72°F (20–22°C). Water Dragons like a large water dish and sturdy branches on which to climb and sun bathe (bask). Full-spectrum lighting is also very important for its valuable UV benefits, helping lizards and plants to develop healthily. A substrate of chunky wood chips, logs, and dense areas of real or plastic plants will help to create the right conditions for your pet.

Handling

Water Dragons are suitable for occasional handling. They can remain static for long periods but are liable to shoot off every now and again.

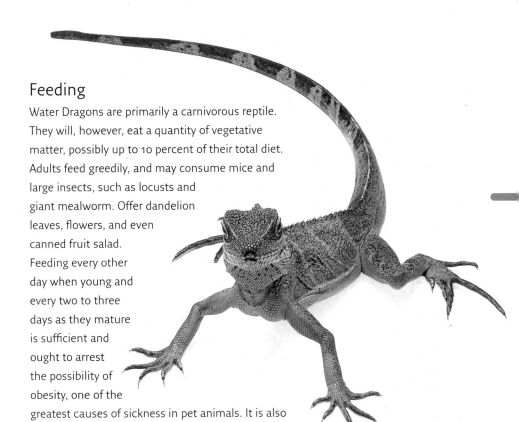

Feeding

Water Dragons are primarily a carnivorous reptile. They will, however, eat a quantity of vegetative matter, possibly up to 10 percent of their total diet. Adults feed greedily, and may consume mice and large insects, such as locusts and giant mealworm. Offer dandelion leaves, flowers, and even canned fruit salad. Feeding every other day when young and every two to three days as they mature is sufficient and ought to arrest the possibility of obesity, one of the greatest causes of sickness in pet animals. It is also advisable to supplement the diet of captive Dragons with a reptile multivitamin product.

Mist spraying is enjoyed and a large water dish should always be available. Dragons will bathe and drink from this, but are also likely to soil it, especially when you've just cleaned it out. Thorough regular cleaning is therefore essential. The water-soiling habit does eventually benefit the keeper as the substrate stays clean for long periods of time.

Magnificent Water Dragons love to climb, jump, and splash around their vivarium. They will grow to around 28 inches (70 cm.) long.

Breeding

Given space, a good environment and diet, Water Dragons are easy to breed. Females will lay up to 20 eggs, which should hatch around 70 days later at 82–88°F (28–30°C). These are usually incubated in vermiculite.

Plumed Basilisk *Basiliscus plumifrons*

Few lizards are as magnificently adorned as the Basilisk, with its yellow eyes and bright green crests. Large males are armored with a large crest on the head, along the back (dorsal crest), and on the tail. These are vibrant green, often marked with rows of blue spots.

The feet of all reptiles will suit the environment in which they live. Compare this Basilisk's foot with one of a Gecko, Chameleon, or Monitor to see how differently they are adapted for their lifestyle.

Habitat

Plumed Basilisks are found in Costa Rica, Panama, and Nicaragua. Athletic sprinters, they can run at speeds of 18 mph over short distances and can take flight in an instant. They can even run across water, hence the name "Jesus lizards" locally. Expect your pet to live about 10 years and grow to 30 inches (75 cm.).

Creating the right environment

Plumed Basilisks require spacious accommodation. A juvenile needs a 36 x 12 x 18-inch (90 x 30 x 45-cm.) vivarium, and most keepers eventually make a custom-built unit about 6 feet 8 inches (2 m.) long and 5 feet (1.5 m.) tall to house adults. To thrive, males should be housed individually or they will fight. Several females may be kept with a single male.

Basilisks enjoy daytime temperatures of 75–86°F (24–30°C), falling at night to 68–75°F (20–24°C). Humidity should about 70–85 percent, so mist spray every other day. A large water bowl is essential, as is a background of real or plastic plants with a sturdy branch beside or over the water. Other branches for climbing and basking on are appreciated, and Basilisks will climb high to catch some rays or flying insects. Some shelter should be provided—cork logs are ideal as retreats.

Handling

If handled regularly, Basilisks can become tame, but they are generally kept for their appearance. Never handle one outside; like many lizards, they can sit as still as a stone one second and then take off at great speed with no warning.

Feeding

Basilisks are fond of most medium and large insects. They benefit from eating small rodents (pink or fuzzy mice). Some plant material is also eaten and any foods considered suitable for omnivorous or herbivorous reptiles can be offered once or twice a week.

Breeding

Basilisks are easy to breed, provided you have the space to house a trio or more, such as one male housed alongside several females. Good nutrition will keep females in optimum condition, and they may lay several clutches of 15–20 eggs per year. Eggs separately incubated in vermiculite take about 70 days to hatch. Juveniles need separating soon afterward and require a well-supplemented diet.

must know

The basilisk's feet are remarkably adapted to enable them to avoid predators. They have delicate, enlarged flaps of scaled skin along the digits on the hind feet. On the downward movement of the foot upon water, these flaps open and, like a webbed foot, exert a greater resistance to the water. At great speed, without sinking, they can literally walk on water.

This recently hatched captive-bred juvenile is ready for its new home. It still lacks the fine crest and colors it will develop as an adult.

Green Iguana *Iguanao iguana*

Iguanas are large tree-climbing lizards that graze on leaves, fruit, and flowers in lush tropical habitats. They reach 64 inches (160 cm.) long and can live for 10 to 15 years. They are generally green, but a huge variety of colors and patterns can be found in different populations within their range, and within subspecies.

must know

The family *Iguanidae* is a large one, and virtually all the members are found in the tropical Americas and are egg layers. Among the iguana clan are the diminutive Anoles, the amazing looking American Horned Lizards, and, of course, the Green and Rhinoceros Iguana.

Habitat

Giant Green Iguanas are native to the tropical Central and South Americas, where they prefer living in the vicinity of lakes, rivers, or the sea. These lizards bask in the sun on branches that overhang the water, sometimes at considerable heights, and, if disturbed, they drop into the water below. Iguanas are good climbers, swimmers, divers, and runners.

Creating the right environment

These truly magnificent reptiles are suitable only for pet owners who have the considerable space required to keep them as they grow. Iguanas need more space as they mature, height being the most important consideration. At the minimum, a juvenile needs a 37 x 15 x 15-inch (92 x 38 x 38-cm.) vivarium, whereas an adult will need a custom-made unit that is at least 48 x 72 x 48 inches (120 x 180 x 120 cm.). Increasingly, iguana owners use small rooms or walk-in vivaria, incorporating the sliding double glass doors that are available at home improvement centers. Iguanas should always be kept individually.

For substrate, use wood chips, leaf litter, pebbles, or any similar material, including Reptile Grass—a

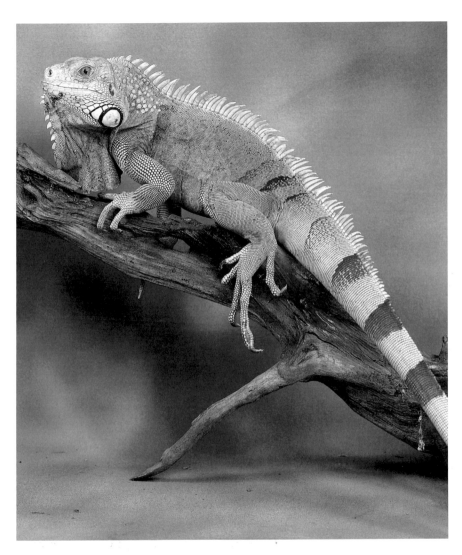

type of Astroturf—and newspaper. Provide sturdy branches for climbing and basking on, and plastic plants for shade, plus a large non-spillable water bowl. Cork logs make good retreats. Delicate planting is not an option for this living dinosaur, which would quickly destroy real plants. A good hot basking spot

Iguanas are well equipped for an arboreal lifestyle. A long fourth finger and toe aid gripping and climbing. The muscular tail is an excellent tool for balance and helps propel diving or swimming Iguanas through the water.

at 86°F (30°C) is needed, and a full-spectrum tube
or basking bulb is essential for maintaining your
lizard's long-term health. Iguanas will enjoy being
mist sprayed immensely, but make sure that the
vivarium does not get too damp.

Handling

Tame iguanas may be walked on a lead or even
perched on a shoulder, but most never become tame
to this extent. Their claws grow long and can lacerate
human flesh, so trim them occasionally, being careful
to avoid the quick, the living part of the claw.

Less tame individuals will need professional
restraining—use long leather gauntlets to protect
yourself. Hold the iguana firmly behind the neck
and above the rear legs, tucking the tail under your
arm to avoid its painful whip. In fact, an irritated
iguana will readily whip, and this can really hurt its
keeper. Young specimens are likely to drop their
tails for defensive reasons, but this ability is lost
once they mature.

Feeding and diet

Adult iguanas are herbivorous, and they will eat a
wide variety, and quantity, of foods. Every other day
or so, you should offer your pet a large bowl filled
with a mixture of fruit, leaves, and vegetables.
Remove the food bowl on the second day and make
sure that you replace it with fresh food, at the very
latest, on the third day.

Juveniles will eat much the same thing but in a
smaller, more finely chopped form. They also need
some live foods, such as crickets, locust hoppers,
and waxworms. Taming and feeding your iguana go

hand-in-hand, and you need to invest considerable time in this process, so that you can both enjoy a good relationship. Provide your pet with a large water bowl to drink from. Iguanas tend to defecate into it, so ensure that it is changed and thoroughly cleaned every other day. They also enjoy being mist sprayed, especially when shedding.

Breeding

Iguanas are farmed in Central America and bred in zoos and institutions in the United States and elsewhere. Captive breeding occurs only in extremely large enclosures. It is unlikely for most pets and, indeed, as they grow too large for their vivaria, many await rehousing or end up in the local zoo or wildlife parks. Home breeding is not recommended.

However, if your pet does breed, up to 40 eggs are deposited by the female over several hours and, after burying them, they are left to incubate in the warm soil. Under optimum conditions they will hatch about 10–15 weeks later, and the youngsters spend the first months of life chasing invertebrates and feeding on leaves and flowers.

These magnificent creatures are suitable only for those pet keepers with the considerable space and time to tame and care for them adequately.

Spur-Thighed Tortoise *Testudo graeca*

These hardy creatures are native to the Mediterranean and are found in Spain, Greece, and Turkey. They become very tame and recognize their keepers. More suitable for an enclosure than a vivarium, these tortoises require considerable space to thrive.

must know

Thousands of tortoises are bred every year in captivity in the United States and elsewhere. A captive-bred baby measuring 3 inches (7.5 cm.) is an ideal acquisition. At first, keep it in a vivarium indoors in winter, and in an outside enclosure in summer. The shell color can vary from yellow to black and they reach 8 inches (20 cm.) in shell length.

Creating the right environment

For all but the youngest juveniles, which need to be penned, tortoises may be kept in a walled or fenced yard for much of the spring and summer months when the yard is frost free. A hutch provides shelter from rain and excesses of temperature. It should have a heater pad or lamp to keep chills at bay and to enable the tortoise to be active on cooler days. Locate the hutch in a sheltered spot, away from direct wind and sunlight. Ensure that ponds and other deep water features are fenced off to prevent your tortoise from drowning.

Despite its reputation, a healthy tortoise is a fast creature, which will crash through flower beds to smell plants before trying them. In the morning, tortoises like to orientate themselves toward the sun, and a south-facing slope is appreciated to help catch those all-important rays. They soon learn the location of their hutches, the best sun-bathing spots, and favored places to rest, feed, or sleep.

Handling

Tortoises can be held firmly from either side, with your thumbs on top of the shell and your fingers underneath the body, but rarely is there a need to handle them. Tortoises tame quickly and will come to you, especially when they are offered tasty titbits. The tendency for their head to be withdrawn will gradually decrease as they become used to you.

Feeding

The Spur-Thighed Tortoise is a herbivore and will be satisfied with most fruit and vegetable matter you offer. Vitamin/mineral supplements should be added to food to promote healthy shell formation, although access to some grazing in a yard and exposure to sunlight will usually fulfill most vitamin and mineral requirements.

Consider offering the following chopped foods, making sure you provide a good selection: beans, carrot, cress, peas, calabrese, lamb's lettuce, cauliflower, cucumber, sweet potato, and berries. They can also forage—I positively encourage dandelions, a favourite tortoise food. Food preferences will vary, but experience will help to

If kept under the right conditions, a captive-bred tortoise should live for at least 30 to 50 years.

guide you. Lettuce should only be a small percentage of your tortoise's diet, no matter how much your pet enjoys it, because it is of low nutritional value. Although normally herbivorous, tortoises seem to enjoy a small amount of meat. Be careful not to overfeed on meat and restrict it to one to five percent of their total diet.

Since tortoises hail from the world's naturally arid environments, most of the moisture they need comes from the foods they consume. However, during very hot, dry periods, additional water may be needed and tepid water can be dribbled or poured over your pet's head. They may then take the opportunity to drink a small amount. Alternatively, you may offer your pet tortoise some water in a shallow dish.

Breeding

The female has a shorter tail and a flat underside, while the male has a longer tail and a concave underside, which enables him to mount the female for mating. The best male/female ratio for breeding tortoises is one male to three or four females. By ramming his shell against hers and biting, the male will force her to give up trying to escape and enable mating to take place. This rough courtship can cause considerable distress and injury to the female.

Eggs are buried about 6 inches (15 cm.) deep in the soil and are so well covered by the female that, unless egg laying is actually witnessed, it may be impossible to locate the site. The eggs must be removed, without turning, and placed in vermiculite at between 82°F (28°C) and 88°F

This captive bred juvenile is being held carefully using two hands. Tortoises need to be firmly supported when carried. It is best to transport them in a sturdy box.

(32°C) at a relative humidity of 70 percent. Hopefully, the eggs will hatch approximately 75–85 days later.

For their first year of life, keep baby tortoises in an indoor vivarium under full-spectrum light at 77–82°F (25–28°C). Move them to small, contained runs in the yard during the warmest months, where access to real ultraviolet rays will help with healthy shell formation. At this stage, they are still vulnerable, so be aware of possible predators.

Hibernation

Hibernation is a natural feature of the European tortoise, and in temperate climates they need to be hibernated to avoid death from the extreme cold if kept outside. Some people bring their tortoises inside into large vivariums to allow them a rest period without actually cooling them or stopping them feeding, and this is an option. Hibernation is a natural process, however, and by gradually cooling your tortoise over a couple of weeks and stopping him eating, the digestive tract will be emptied. I hibernate mine in a ventilated box in loose dry compost covered in straw and placed ina cool area with a stable temperature of around 37–45°F (3–7°C). Essentially, tortoises need gradual cooling, storing within a stable temperature range, and checking regularly in case they are active. It is not recommended to hibernate baby tortoises until they have a plastron (shell) length of around 5 inches (13 cm.). Do some research if you have never hibernated one before, because conditions vary from region to region.

want to know more?

• Thousands of books are available about reptiles in general and lizards and tortoises in particular. Look in your local library.
• A good web portal leading to articles, photographs, and other web sites on reptiles is www.kingsnake.com
• Wherever you live in the world, you should be able to find local reptile or tortoise groups. Check your local library or community news for more information.

4 Reptiles: Snakes

Snakes are not only beautiful creatures but many are also remarkably friendly and easy to care for. Increasingly popular as pets, they are essentially low-maintenance animals that fit in well with modern lifestyles. Cheap to keep, with some adult supervision snakes are suitable for all age groups. Considerably less time-consuming than more conventional pets, most species make no noise, don't smell, and cannot cause allergic reactions. As a good owner, it is your responsibility to ensure that the vivarium conditions are correct for your new pet to thrive. Your own preference and domestic situation should dictate what type of snake is most suited to you and your family.

What are snakes?

All snakes are reptiles and each and every one is a predator that consumes its prey whole. They are unable to chew or break their food into pieces, and this, in its way, makes the feeding of snakes for the pet keeper a relatively simple affair.

Habitats

In the wild, snakes naturally inhabit a wide range of environments, from open sea to deserts, woodland and even treetops. All snakes need to thermoregulate and rely entirely on their environment to satisfy their need for warmth. They may bask in the sun or coil up by a warm rock in order to heat up and become active. To avoid becoming too hot, they will also at times retreat into a den or burrow to cool down.

Physiology

Snakes have, in the distant past, evolved from lizards and are, in effect, specially modified limbless lizards. Periodic sloughing replaces their old skin, and it is always discarded, instead of consumed, which occurs among many lizards and frogs. Their elongated skeleton consists of up to 400 separate vertebrae, mostly attached to long curved ribs. The usual vertebrate organs, including the heart, liver, stomach, and lungs, are also elongated and protected by the extended rib cage.

Senses

While snakes entirely lack an external ear and ear drum, they pick up airborne and earthborne sound vibrations along the body and through a small inner ear bone adjacent to the lower jaw. However, their main sensory organ is the forked tongue, which, flickering up and down and in and out, gathers tiny particles and pulls them back into the mouth. They are analyzed by a structure in the roof of the mouth called the Jacobsons organ, which, in effect, smells and tastes the environment for the snake.

Scales

Snakes are covered in scales, which are hardened parts of the skin forming a protective outer covering and help to prevent desiccation. Scales vary in size and shape, with larger, wide (ventral) scales found on the belly, and smaller ones along the body. While different species have different numbers and arrangements of scales, an individual's scales may grow as it matures, but it will not gain nor lose the actual number of scales throughout its life. Snakes lack eyelids and cannot close their eyes, which are protected by a transparent (spectacle) scale.

The coloration of snakes is highly variable. Many have tones and patterns enabling them to blend in with their natural habitat. Others may use bright colors as a warning, including this Milk Snake that is a mimic— pretending to be dangerous.

Californian Kingsnake
Lampropeltis getulus californiae

Thousands of beautifully patterned Kingsnakes are bred every year by hobbyists specifically for the pet trade. They are ideal pets in that they tend to enjoy handling, prefer small, secure caging, and rarely development ailments or loss of appetite.

must know

Kingsnakes live in a range of habitats, from forests to deserts, and they may be found in the suburbs of some cities, in parks and yards. They are an American species occurring over a large range from Canada in the north to Ecuador in the south.

Fierce predators

In their wild state, the Kingsnake is an aggressive and opportunistic predator, taking a large range of prey from lizards, birds, and rodents, to other American snakes mentioned in this book. They are called Kingsnakes because they will actively catch, kill, and consume even highly venomous snakes, making them, understandably, the "king of snakes" and a tolerated backyard snake in areas where dangerous snakes may also be found. Growing to about 4 feet (1.2 m.) long, this medium-size reptile should live for at least 10–15 years.

Subspecies

Several subspecies (closely related) exist and can be cared for in much the same way. Each has different patterns and coloration. Look out for the following:

- Florida King (*Lampropeltis getulus floridana*)
- Mexican Black King (*Lampropeltis getulus nigritus*)
- Speckled Kingsnake (*Lampropeltis getulus holbrooki*)
  While most Californian Kingsnakes appear banded with black-and-white hoops, striped forms are also available. Because they are increasingly interbred in captivity, a wide variety of colored and patterned forms are becoming available.

Creating the right environment

Because Kingsnakes will eat other snakes (ophiophagous) they must be kept separately, even as juveniles, or you risk suddenly losing one of your pets. A clean dry vivarium, 36 x 12 x 12 inches (90 x 30 x 30 cm.), is more than adequate for an adult. A temperature gradient ranging from 75–86°F (24–30°C) is ideal.

Kingsnakes are not great climbers but it is worth giving them the option by providing a branch or two in the vivarium. Suggested furnishings would include a base substrate of paper, bark chips, leaf litter, or a mixture of the above. Water should always be available for them and regularly changed. Occasional mist spraying is beneficial, as would be the inclusion of a humidity box.

In the wild, Californian Kingsnakes are usually either banded, like the one above, or striped, where the black-and-white markings run along the length of the body. The darker markings range from jet black to a chocolate color. The white markings are also variable, from creamy yellow to pure white.

Handling

The sooner you get to know each other the better for both of you. Kingsnakes should be at least part tame and definitely proven feeders before being

This glossy Mexican Black Kingsnake (*Lampropeltis getulus nigrities*) is in excellent overall condition; its scales are shiny and it is not too fat, nor too thin.

purchased from a dealer. The very young are initially snappy and strike out, rapidly vibrating their tails as a threat defense posture—they have yet to learn that you mean no harm. However, Kingsnakes soon tame and will rarely offend their keeper by biting once they are conditioned to regular handling.

Feeding

Kingsnakes tend to feed well and the domestic mouse is all that they need as a diet for a healthy life. Most snakes are very hungry after a slough but they may refuse food just beforehand.

Without overfeeding them, allow a Kingsnake as much as it can eat in about 10 minutes every six to eight days on average. However, most snakes eat very regularly for some time, then, as they are "fed up," they will refuse food for a while, particularly during a colder or winter/darker phase of the year.

Don't worry—this is perfectly normal snake behavior. So much of our mammalian time is based on and around eating food that it takes some time for us to understand food from a reptile's perspective. This often consists of long periods with nothing to eat, followed by a sudden feast, but rarely any regular week-by-week feeding.

A multi-kill capacity

Unlike most snakes, which catch and constrict individual prey, the Kingsnakes have developed a multi-kill capacity, and, on finding a nest of rodents, for example, they can take one by the mouth but still hold and crush others within their coils and against the ground or burrow walls. This allows them to feast in times of plenty, so they can survive periods of scarce food availability. Of course, with pet snakes feeding on dead food, this phenomenon is rarely witnessed, but try offering your snake two dead mice at once and see what happens.

Breeding

These snakes are most likely to mate after a period of hibernation. They should be kept for several weeks, without any feeding, at temperatures of around 54–60°F (12–15°C). After this period, raise the temperature to their normal vivarium conditions (see page 121). When ready for mating, usually after a slough, the female releases hormones to attract the male. Mating snakes should be watched to ensure that one does not eat the other.

Return the female to her vivarium. Insert a laying container to provide a secure and comfortable spot in which to lay her eggs. About five to seven weeks after mating, between 5 and 17 eggs will be laid, each measuring up to 2 inches (5 cm.) long and 1 inch (2 cm.) wide. These should then be removed and incubated in vermiculite at 75°F (24°C).

Within 70 days, the eggs will hatch into 10-inch (25-cm.) long babies. Once sloughing has taken place, usually 12–16 days after birth, the young snakes will be ready to feed on the smallest of pinkies. At around four to six months of age, Californian Kingsnakes are an ideal purchase as a pet. This species of snake matures at two-and-a-half to three years.

watch out!

Most snake keepers will, at some time, usually by accident, get bitten. Apart from the initial shock, your snake is unlikely to cause itself or you much damage. Never put your hands close to a snake if you've been handling its food. You can't blame it for biting you if you wave around mouse-scented fingers. Antiseptic cream should be all that is required, and a bandage for your bruised ego.

This chocolate-and-banana colored Californian Kingsnake is one of the numerous color morphs produced by breeders.

Sinloan Milk Snake
Lampropeltis triangulum sinaloae

Among the most beautiful of all pet reptiles, these bright, small snakes are widely available. Milk Snake is a term given to the smaller and more colorful members of the Kingsnake group. There are 25 recognized subspecies.

must know

Sinloan Milk Snakes have tricolored bands of black, white, and red along the length of their body. The red or orange bands are particularly wide in this pencil-slim Mexican species, and the snakes have a small black snout.

Habitat and behavior

Milk Snakes inhabit the same types of habitat as Kingsnakes, but their range extends a little further north and south in the Americas. They range in size considerably, with those in the north tending to be smaller than their relatives from warmer countries in South America. *Lampropeltis triangulum micropholis* from Costa Rica and parts of South America can grow to 5 feet (1.5 m.). The Sinloan Milk Snake reaches up to 40 inches (1 m.) in length but is usually smaller, averaging 24 inches (60 cm.).

Wild Milk Snakes are usually crepuscular/nocturnal creatures, but, in the security of the home they may be active at any time. However, they tend to spend much of their time secreted away in a hiding place. Wild Milk Snakes catch and eat small prey animals, such as lizards, rodents, and even other Milk Snakes; for this reason, it is recommended that individual snakes are housed separately.

Creating the right environment

All Milk Snakes require virtually identical care, with the larger species in more spacious accommodation. The small Sinloan Milk Snake is best kept in a small 24 x 12 x 12-inch (60 x 30 x 30-cm.) secure

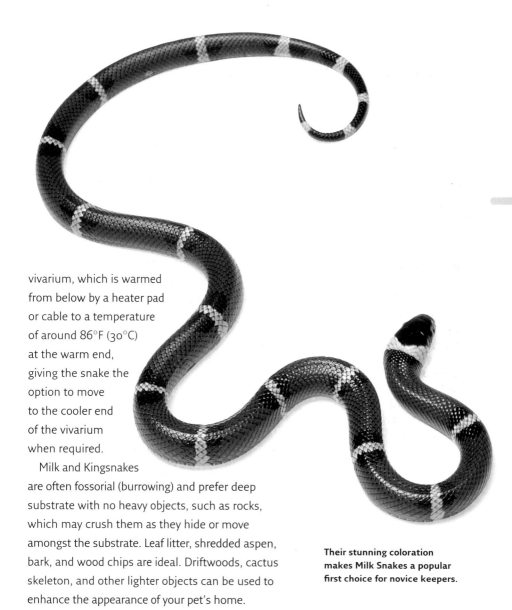

vivarium, which is warmed from below by a heater pad or cable to a temperature of around 86°F (30°C) at the warm end, giving the snake the option to move to the cooler end of the vivarium when required.

Milk and Kingsnakes are often fossorial (burrowing) and prefer deep substrate with no heavy objects, such as rocks, which may crush them as they hide or move amongst the substrate. Leaf litter, shredded aspen, bark, and wood chips are ideal. Driftwoods, cactus skeleton, and other lighter objects can be used to enhance the appearance of your pet's home.

These snakes do not like to be damp, and thus only a small water dish is required. A small humidity chamber can also be of benefit to assist shedding. A secure purpose-built vivarium is essential because these snakes are slight in build and great escapers.

Their stunning coloration makes Milk Snakes a popular first choice for novice keepers.

must know

Named after the English naturalist H. W. Bates, Batesian mimicry is where an edible and otherwise unprotected species, such as the Milk Snake, closely resembles a dangerous species—in this case, Coral Snakes. This evolution has occurred as a strategy to avoid predation, so the harmless Milk Snake falsely advertises itself as a dangerous animal instead of relying on camouflage and blending in with its habitat.

Handling

Most Milk Snakes become tame and easy to handle without any problems. When they are first handled, they can be a bit jerky in their movements but are fine for calmer hands. If you are unused to snake handling, sit down before you start—you would not want to accidentally drop a snake.

Snakes are less likely to tolerate handling during the first couple of days after feeding, and a nervous or scared snake may regurgitate food or even defecate on you. However, patience, persistence, and common sense will help tame most snakes in a matter of weeks. Even if early on in your relationship, your snake does bite, it has such a tiny mouth that it can hardly do much harm.

Feeding

Rarely posing any feeding problems, Milk Snakes tend to prefer several smaller items instead of one very large one. Feed as often as any other Kingsnake, being careful that no substrate is taken in alongside meals. By simply placing their food on a piece of paper substrate, ingestion problems can easily be avoided. As with all snakes, feeding in separate containers is always advised (see page 122).

Your newly acquired Milk Snake should soon be settled into a diet of pinkies. Baby snakes will usually begin to feed after their first slough at about 10-14 days. They should then be offered two to three small pinkies at a sitting, once every five to six days. At several months of age (when they are best purchased as pets), they can be offered several pinkies or fuzzies—as much as they will consume in about 10 minutes—every seven to ten days.

Once adult, feed your snake as much as can be eaten in 10–15 minutes, every six to eight days. The food a snake consumes should leave a visible, but not abnormal-size, swelling along its body. You may find that after feeding well for a month or more your pet snake may refuse food for a number of weeks. However, do not worry if this happens—it is simply full and this is normal.

Breeding

These snakes are not sexually dimorphic, so there is no easy way for us to sex them. Most snakes will be sexed by the breeder or dealer who is supplying the specimen. For breeding information, see the section on Kingsnakes (see page 122), but, generally speaking, a cooling period or a "brumation," as herpetologists now call it, is a good idea before any breeding is attempted. A typical clutch would be between 5 and 18 eggs. If incubated in some vermiculite at 75°F (24°C), they should hatch around 60 days later.

Juvenile Milk Snakes are usually reared in small containers that will give them all their basic requirements, including heat, humidity, and a sense of security.

Corn Snake *Elaphe guttata guttata*

Any attractive snake with a good temperament that feeds well and is easy to breed in captivity is likely to be popular as a pet; such is the Corn Snake. These colorful snakes are native to the warmer parts of the United States, and are among the most popular species for first-time keepers and more experienced herpers.

must know

A medium-size snake will measure between 32 inches (80 cm.) and 5 feet (1.5 m.). They can breed from about two years of age and live as a pet for 10-15 years, stopping breeding by about six years of age— their probable maximum natural wild lifespan.

Habitat and appearance

Corn Snakes are agile hunters, named after the corn fields and stores in which they search for rodent prey. Great climbers and burrowers, they can scale a tree trunk or root about under straw or hay with equal skill. With captive breeding, many color phases or morphs are routinely available, and juvenile Corn Snakes may be bought with names such as Black Corn, Sun-kissed, Caramel, or Zigzag, all referring to their color or patterns. Its wild natural coloration is blotched with burnt orange or red saddles, ringed in black over a tangerine background. The belly scales are frequently checkered black and white.

Creating the right environment

Corn Snakes require a warm, dry vivarium with an average temperature range of 77-86°F (25-30°C), cooling slightly in winter to about 68°F (20°C). An adult pair should be provided with a 36 x 24 x 24-inch (90 x 60 x 60-cm.) vivarium. Newly hatched and juvenile individual snakes need smaller, more secure units, such as a 10 x 4 x 4 inches (25 x 10 x 10 cm.) or a 24 x 12 x 12-inch (60 x 30 x 30-cm.) vivarium.

Any decorations should be thoroughly cleaned before placing in the vivarium, especially leaf litter, which may introduce some unwanted pests into the snake's home. The overnight freezing of leaves will ensure that most potential pests, such as mites or ticks, are killed. The vivarium is simple to furnish becuase this snake is equally at home in woodland, pasture, a barn, or a hole in a tree trunk. So logs, stones, cork logs, leaf litter, bark chips, and climbing branches can all be used to decorate the vivarium for your viewing, and also to provide plenty of climbing areas, as well as secure retreats for your pet.

Water, in a shallow dish, should be available at all times. As for most reptiles, this snake appreciates a periodic mist spraying almost as much as a humidity chamber. As you gain experience of keeping snakes and learn to recognize how dry or humid a vivarium is and how to maintain a good balance between too little and too much humidity (air moisture), you can dispense with humidity chambers altogether. However, for many reptiles they are an invaluable aid to improving the quality of their lives and adding an element of comfort.

Corn Snakes will need access to fresh water for drinking and will really enjoy the occasional bath. Increased humidity helps snakes slough without difficulty.

Regular handling of juvenile snakes will condition them to human contact—they soon learn that contact will not harm them.

Handling

Corn Snakes rarely prove difficult to handle, but they are agile and can soon slip inside a sofa or under a floorboard. I find that these snakes prefer being approached from front-opening instead of top-opening vivaria. To a snake, there is something particularly threatening about sudden "predatory" movements from above.

Baby snakes are usually very defensive to begin with and will hiss and strike out at anything that moves. Regular handling at this stage will condition or tame it to realize that humans mean no harm. Indeed, we are soon recognized as a good source of both warmth and food. Once it is being handled, the snake should calm down, and as it starts to feed

Attractive colorations and good temperament make these snakes a popular choice of pet.

over a few weeks it changes from a nervous baby snake to a more relaxed juvenile.

Feeding

Juveniles may be offered several pinkies or fuzzies once every seven to ten days. Adults will require two to three adult mice every two weeks. About 60 small rodents will be needed in the first year of life, on average, making snakes surprisingly cheap to keep in comparison to some other pet animals. Be flexible with feeding —Corn Snakes' appetites will vary—but try to avoid overindulging them because they will rarely refuse a feed.

Breeding

Breeding usually takes place during spring, and mating is characterized by an intertwined embrace. Mating in snakes provides an ideal opportunity to watch an ancient but effective reproductive process. A keen male will follow a prospective female around the vivarium, often biting her and rubbing against the length of her body. Eventually he will bite her firmly on the neck and put the weight of his body on top of hers. He will stimulate her by rubbing and making wavelike motions against her cloacal region and mating will take place. Courtship and mating can last for several hours.

Up to 20 eggs are laid in a concealed spot in the soil—suitable places are under a dish or log, or in a hide box. The eggs should be incubated in vermiculite at 82-86°F (28-30°C). They will hatch after around ten weeks. Corn Snakes mature at two to three years, when they are about 32 inches (80 cm.) long, and can breed until they are about ten years of age.

must know

Most male snakes have longer tails than the females. You can measure similarly aged snakes from the vent to the tail tip to ascertain the correct sex.

Yellow Rat Snake *Elaphe obsoleta quadrivittata*

The Yellow Rat Snake is a familiar and harmless snake that is regularly found close to human habitation in the eastern United States, in parts of Florida, Georgia, and Carolina. A close relative of the Corn Snake, it is just as easy to keep in captivity and is widely available from captive-bred stocks.

must know

Laying many eggs is a survival strategy for reptiles. Snakes rarely offer any parental care of their young, which fend for themselves as soon as they are born or hatch from an egg. Having many babies, like the Yellow Rat Snake's 44 young, increases the chance that some will survive to adulthood.

Creating the right environment

A large snake, an adult can reach 80 inches (2 m.) or more, but it still prefers secure rather than spacious accommodation. A 48 x 36 x 18-inch (120 x 90 x 45-cm.) vivarium will suit a pair of snakes. With a temperature range of 77–86°F (25–30°C), they are frequently kept or bred by herpetologists in remarkably small and plain breeding units with paper as a substrate, a hide box, and a water bowl.

This climbing (arboreal) snake enjoys some height and even elevated logs or a shelf to rest on and hide in. However, if you only have one or two snakes to look after, then you may prefer to establish a more naturalistic, attractive-looking vivarium. A large range of both natural and artificial materials are suitable to decorate it. As long as it is warm and can hide, the Rat Snake will remain unaffected by the simplicity or effort taken in decoration.

Handling

Initially very wild, baby Rat Snakes soon tame and are a popular snake for handling. Most snakes should not be handled for several days just after a feed. Some do not mind, but others prefer to be left alone to let the digestion of food in peace.

Feeding

Often referred to as chicken snakes in the United States, adult Rat Snakes will consume many prey items, including chicks and chicken eggs as well as mice, bats and other rodents, and birds. Juveniles in the wild are more likely to take frogs and lizards. However, as pets they are happy to accept defrosted pinkies. These greedy snakes are unlikely to ever become difficult to feed.

This impressive and potentially powerful reptile is highly variable in coloration, ranging from yellows to orange.

Breeding

While many snakes are adversely affected by land development, farming, housing, and forest clearance, Rat Snakes seem to thrive and their populations tend to increase when living alongside mankind. Saw mills, barns, and log piles all offer ideal hunting territory, and compost or sawdust are utilized as egg-laying sites. Between 5 and 44 eggs are laid after mating in the spring. Hatchlings, 12 inches (30 cm.) long, lack the distinctive stripes seen on adults. Their patchy pattern fades as they mature into adults over the first 12–16 months. The Latin *obsoletus* (worn out) refers to this gradual fading.

must know

This primarily diurnal snake is a true natural-born killer and is of significant agricultural importance, capable of eating large numbers of pest rodents.

House Snake *Lamprophis fuliginosus*

These slim chocolate brown snakes are a common African species and are frequently found in, under, or near houses in villages and towns. In the wild, they feed mainly on rodents and lizards. Although not as common or as colorful as Corn and King Snakes, they are small and easy to keep and breed.

must know

House Snakes are highly recommended for the novice keeper because they are rated as an easy-to-handle species and two or more can be kept together. They live for up to 15 years and can grow to 45 inches (112 cm.), but 24 inches (60 cm.) is more usual.

Creating the right environment

These snakes are best kept in a dry, woodland-style setup or just on plain paper. Shredded Aspen is great, but wood chips and leaves are more decorative. Some suitable hiding places of natural material or store-bought retreats are essential, because House Snakes love hiding. A pair or, better still, a trio of one male and two females should be housed in a 36 x 18 x 15-inch (90 x 45 x 38-cm.) vivarium.

Water should always be available and a container with moist moss or sprayed plastic plants should be used as a humidity chamber. Provide a temperature range of around 77–82°F (25–28°C).

Secure and content within their shelter, juvenile House Snakes spend much of their time hiding.

Handling

Start to handle your snake as soon as you get it. House Snakes are, in my opinion, well suited to handling as a pet although, like many other species, they may bite or strike at sudden movements.

Feeding

These greedy snakes always seem to be hungry and are capable of taking large prey in relation to their head and neck size. In general, as a guide, hatchlings should be fed several small pinkies every three to four days; juveniles around two to three fuzzies every six to eight days; and adults one to three adult mice every 10–14 days. However, some snakes will have smaller or larger appetites.

Breeding

Breeding is likely without adjusting the temperature or light cycles, as is required in many other species. House Snakes breed from around a year old, with the female laying 8–15 eggs per clutch. Incubate them at 80°F (27°C) for about 60 days, when the babies will hatch, at 8 inches (20.5 cm.) long. After a week, they shed and are ready to feed on small pinkies, at which point separate them to avoid fighting over food. Raise them in small secure containers or pet homes until big enough to adapt to a larger vivarium.

Being a small species, House Snakes only require a moderate-size vivarium and make a good introduction to snake keeping.

Ball Python *Python regius*

I recommend this attractive species as an excellent choice of pet snake, especially for beginners. Reaching a maximum length of 6 feet 8 inches (2 m.), but often smaller, Ball Pythons are never too large to become unmanageable and have a great temperament.

Habitat
Native to West African grasslands and forest clearings, these snakes are solitary terrestrial creatures frequently inhabiting mammal burrows. Hunting mainly at night and during the early hours of morning and evening (crepuscular), they catch gerbil-like rodents for most of their diet.

Creating the right environment
You will need a vivarium measuring 48 x 18 x 18 inches (120 x 45 x 45 cm) for keeping a pair of adults or several juvenile pythons. Initially, a baby python may prefer a much smaller pet home—snakes often feel much more secure in small spaces, at least until they begin to grow and settle in. Several Ball Pythons can be kept together safely, but if kept alone they will not get lonely.

Enjoying fresh air, a Ball Python's housing should always be well ventilated and heated within a 75–86°F (24–30°C) range. These snakes really enjoy their shelters and will frequently lie coiled within a cork log or similar bit of vivarium furnishing, with just their head sticking out watching.

A base substrate of newspaper is fine, but bark chips are much more attractive. Leaf litter also adds visual interest and enhances the appearance of

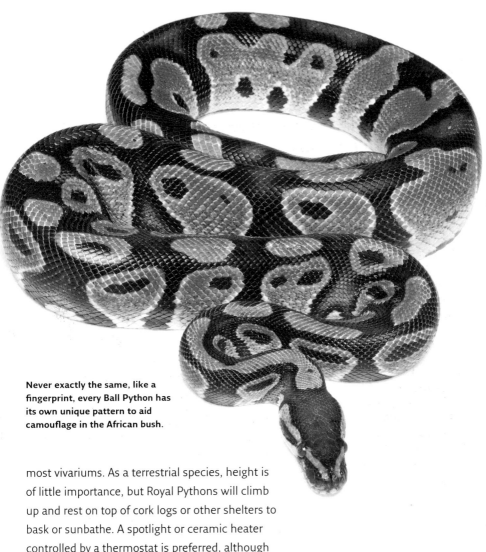

Never exactly the same, like a
fingerprint, every Ball Python has
its own unique pattern to aid
camouflage in the African bush.

most vivariums. As a terrestrial species, height is
of little importance, but Royal Pythons will climb
up and rest on top of cork logs or other shelters to
bask or sunbathe. A spotlight or ceramic heater
controlled by a thermostat is preferred, although
in a warm house heater pads may be sufficient.

Most reptiles, including pythons, will enjoy an
occasional bath. Mist spraying every so often is
recommended, and a humidity chamber placed
within their vivarium should help to prevent
dehydration and ensure regular skin shedding.

Pythons are clean animals, going defecating only
every 10–14 days or so, and hence cleaning is kept

must know

Security is of paramount importance to keep your animals safe and secure. Most herptiles can squeeze through the tiniest gaps. Exo-terra and other modern designer vivaria have a door lock and secure lid. Any cage with glass sliding doors should have a lock or a rubber wedge to keep it secure. Aquaria and vivaria should be placed on a polystyrene base. Use electrical equipment in accordance with the instructions, and fit a circuit breaker for safety.

to a minimum and soiled areas are easily removed. Occasionally, snakes will defecate in their water bowl, so this will need thorough cleaning before being replaced with fresh water. It should be sited away from any heat sources.

Handling

Ball Pythons are easy to handle, but do ensure, as with all pets, that you support much of their body—don't let them just dangle or jerk them around. Most snakes wrap around you when being handled: smaller ones on the hand, wrist and fingers; larger ones on the arms and neck. Ball Pythons are too small to cause any concern unless handled by a very young child. If a Ball, or any snake for that matter, is wrapping too tightly or won't let go, then reach for its tail. Once you have a snake by its tail you are effectively in control and can more easily unwrap the animal than by tugging at the middle of its body. These creatures are shy, cautious even, but often inquisitive when handled.

Feeding

A juvenile Ball Python should be offered foods about once every 6 to 12 days, and adults every 10–14 days. However, if well fed over a period of time, these snakes are likely to refuse food, or even fast for a while, ranging from a couple of weeks up to several months. However, there is no need to be unduly alarmed at this—pythons lead relatively inactive lives and have simply had enough food. In time, particularly after the next slough, feeding will resume. If in doubt about your python, consult a herpetologist, who will probably confirm that it has had plenty to eat and is otherwise in good health. Should you be concerned that your snake is actually sick, you should consult a herptile-familiar veterinarian. A record of its feeding habits will be a great help in any diagnosis.

Breeding

Large numbers of Ball Pythons are bred by hobbyists every year, and they are even available in a range of designer patterns and coloration. Adults are easily sexed by looking at their claws and tails from underneath. The tail and the claws are usually longer in males, with the twinned reproductive organ or hemipenis located below the vent, so a bulge is noticeable. Females can lay from 6 to 14 eggs, but typically 6 to 8, which hatch some 60 days later.

This captive bred baby Ball is learning that its keeper poses no threat; it will be tamed quickly.

Woma or Sand Python *Aspidites ramsayi*

These docile pythons are found only in Australia, occurring across a range of habitats from the harsh, dry desert interior to more wooded coastal areas. They are prolific feeders and breeders and handle easily, making them a popular and sensible choice of medium-size pet snake.

must know

Unlike other pythons, the Woma and Black Headed Python lack the facial heat-sensitive pits that are used to detect prey. Some people speculate, probably correctly, that as they are both predominantly ophiophagous species, the heat pits that help other pythons detect warm-blooded prey may not have evolved in these ancient reptiles.

Appearance and habitat

Womas have small, dark eyes and a narrow head, which gives them a surprisingly unpythonlike appearance. They vary in color from a tawny olive brown through to a milky orange, pink, and red. The body is heavily banded and the scales are both smooth and small. This is a very appealing snake, measuring an average 5 feet (1.5 m.) in length. Some Womas can reach as much as 10 feet (3 m.), depending on which part of Australia the original specimens came from.

Creating the right environment

For an individual adult snake, a 48 x 18 x 18-inch (120 x 45 x 45-cm.) vivarium is ideal. Juveniles prefer smaller accommodation, especially when you are establishing a new purchase. Womas are usually housed alone or, at the very least, they are separated when feeding—like the Black Headed Pythons, they are extremely ophiophagous (snake eating). Vivaria should be well ventilated, and front-access glass sliding doors are recommended. Most pythons are happy to be kept on paper, but shredded aspen, leaf litter, and a host of other substrates can all be utilized to make a more attractive enclosure. Shelters/hides are needed and a temperature gradient, using heating cable/pads or lamps, should offer the snake a 75–95°F (24–35°C) range. Water need be offered only on a weekly basis, and, as always, the occasional mist spraying is appreciated, although humidity levels should be low. Womas, like many pythons, can expect a life span of 20–30 years in captivity.

Initially fetching high prices, Womas are becoming more available and affordable as the captive breeding rates increase.

Inhabiting frequently hostile and arid environments where drought is common, Womas can survive for long periods without either food or water, possibly for a period of up to 12 months or even more in their natural environment.

Unlike most other python species, the head of a Woma is more slender in appearance.

Handling

Womas are sensitive to sudden movements near the head, jerking back if your approach is too direct. Juveniles may be a bit jumpy at first but, like most pythons, soon tame with regular handling. Overall, this is a wonderful snake to keep and handle.

Feeding

This is a gorger of a snake, seemingly always eager to eat and happy to consume mice or small rats. I suggest feeding all snakes outside their home vivarium after a short handling session and in a separate pet home container. This conditions the snake and reduces the chance of it striking hungrily at you when your hand goes in the cage to clean it or offer water. Offer an average two to three mice a week, but more or less depending on the size of your pet. With experience, you will get to know how hungry your snake is likely to be and how much to feed. Always separate Womas when feeding.

Breeding

Like all pythons, Womas are an egg-laying species and seem to breed prolifically. Breeding can be attempted at about two or three years of age. A seasonal or pre-pairing cooling is useful but not essential with this species. Overweight reptiles are less likely to breed successfully than healthy, well-nourished but trim individuals. Females will lay between 5 and 12 eggs per clutch but average around 12. If allowed, they will remain coiled with the eggs until they hatch. The young should be separated as soon as they emerge from the egg, if not before. Young Womas are best reared in smaller containers initially.

When it is tightly coiled, the banded patterning of this West Australian Woma is clearly visible.

Childrens Python *Liasis childreni*

Essentially a small and secretive snake, the Childrens Python is native to most of Northern Australia but absent from the extreme south. This adaptable snake is as likely to be found in coastal forests as inland deserts, preferring to rest in termite mounds, under rock overhangs, or other compact hiding places.

must know

A dark brown stripe behind the eye helps to camouflage this light brown, blotchy python. Underneath the wide belly, the ventral scales are usually a creamy white color. Growing to a maximum of 40 inches (1 m.), this small terrestrial species can live for up to 20 years.

Creating the right environment

An essentially warm and dry environment is key to successful husbandry. Temperatures of 74–86°F (23–30°C) are ideal, and, like many other pythons, a bad chill could be as life threatening as overheating. I recommend the use of both thermometers and thermostats to ensure that adequate but not excessive warmth is always maintained.

A 36 x 15 x 15-inch (90 x 38 x 38-cm.) vivarium is adequate, with a substrate of cork/wood chips. If a larger vivarium be offered, there must be secure, small hiding places available to provide the sense of security these snakes need. Most snakes prefer places they can squeeze into rather than a big cave.

Feeding

Wild Childrens Pythons feed on any small mammal, bird, frog, or lizard they are able to catch. Usually excellent feeders as pets, they take readily to their diet of mice or small rats. A few small mice offered every 10–16 days or so should be sufficient.

Handling

Never growing too large or becoming awkward to handle, these pythons have a good temperament.

Generally a passive species, they are suitable for regular handling by their keepers.

Breeding

The silent male snake is attracted to a female by her smell—a chemical, or pheromone, trail that she leaves for the male to follow. If you do attempt breeding, notice how excited a male snake becomes in the company of a female of the same species. The tongue flicks in and out more frequently, sometimes rapidly, at other times staying extended in long, slow, and rhythmic movements. After stimulating the female by rubbing along the length of her body, the snakes entwine and mating occurs while they are paired. Contentedly mating snakes may be left together for a week or so before being separated, so a gravid female can develop in peace.

Between 10 and 50 eggs can be produced by these prolific pythons. Care for them in a similar way to most other pythons, keeping the incubating moss or vermiculite medium moist but not wet.

Growing to around a 40 inches (1 m.), small pythons, like the Childrens, are easy to handle and may be more suitable as a pet for the beginner.

Black Headed Python
Aspidites melanocephalus

This spectacular-looking snake has an almost purple-black head and neck. Like the Woma, it is banded but more predominantly with creamy white or gray background scales.

must know

Black Headed Pythons are largely terrestrial but may live and hunt up on rocky outcrops or in rodent burrows. From a secure hole or ledge, they expose only their black head to absorb the radiant heat from the sun and thermoregulate effectively without revealing much of their body to potential prey or predators. Dark colors, such as black, absorb heat more effectively than lighter colors.

Habitat and behavior

A muscular snake reaching up to 10 feet (3 m.) but usually smaller, the Black Headed Python inhabits the northern third of the Australian continent over a vast range, living generally in more lush areas where prey is most numerous. It appears that both the Aspidities pythons share common traits. They multi-kill prey by squeezing several mammals at once and catch and eat large venomous snakes—reportedly not always asphyxiating them first but eating them alive—they are immune to the multiple bites from otherwise deadly snakes in the region.

Creating the right environment

A 48 x 18 x 18-inch (120 x 45 x 45-cm.) vivarium is ideal. Snakes should be kept separately and like a dry home with some opportunity to burrow in shredded paper, leaf litter, or a similar substrate. Hiding spaces are appreciated across the heat gradient of the unit—75-95°F (24-35°C) is a good range.

Handling

Captive-reared specimens should pose no problems for handling. Initially they are often hissy but rarely bite, but they may partly open their mouth and push your hand away when nervous. if you acquire a young snake from captive stock, tame it quickly and accustom it to handling from an early age.

Feeding

While captive specimens readily take mice or rats, wild Black Headed Pythons consume small lizards, monitors, mammals, birds, and other snakes. Feed as much as they will eat over 10 minutes or so once every 12 days on average. Larger snakes will prefer rats to mice. They may reject their food if they are given a cooling option seasonally for a few months.

Breeding

The mating of entwined snakes can last for between 20 minutes and six to seven hours or more. Females produce five to ten eggs, which hatch two to three months later. These should be incubated in some vermiculite, but some breeders let them stay with the parent coiled around them until they hatch.

A stunning and solid python, Black Heads are one of the more recently seen species available.

Carpet Python *Morelia spilotes variegata*

This attractive medium-size python is common throughout much of the Australian continent and New Guinea. It reaches a rare maximum length of 16 feet 8 inches (5 m.), but this is small in comparison to the longest snake in the world, the Reticulated python (*Python reticularis*) at 30–33 feet (9–10 m.).

must know

The subspecies Diamond Python (*Morelia spilotes spilotes*) derives its name from its pattern of diamondlike marks and reaches 10 feet (3 m.) on average, but specimens over 15 feet (4.5 m.) have been reported.

Habitat and appearance

Carpet Pythons may be found in arid desertlike environments, living in burrows as well as high in the rain forest canopy, using their prehensile tail for extra climbing dexterity. In Australia, they are common around agricultural buildings, attracted by rodents or rabbits. Their markings vary considerably, from a black and gray with blotches and stripes to a high yellow or rusty color. The name apparently comes from the oriental-carpet look of the patterns.

Creating the right environment

These snakes need a large dry vivarium at 74–86°F (23–30°C) with ground and elevated shelters. The base should be covered in paper or wood chips.

Good climbing branches need to be sited at a safe distance from any lightbulbs or ceramic heaters. A heater pad or two on the floor should keep even the largest cages warm but must be carefully monitored with a thermostat. As they mature, snakes should be housed in larger cages or enclosures—around 72 x 24 x 24 inches (180 x 60 x 60 cm.) is adequate for a medium-size specimen. Good ventilation is always important but drafts must be avoided.

Handling

Carpet Pythons are good for handling, but large snakes are never as relaxing to hold as smaller ones. Few big snakes ever settle down on your arm or in your pocket. They tend to reach about or coil too tightly around whatever else is nearby and are less likely to settle down calmly. Many snake keepers enjoy large snakes for the sheer pleasure of watching their behavior and natural beauty.

Feeding

A popular pet species, this impressive snake will eat any bird or mammal offered. My own specimen, a 11-foot 8-inch (3.5-m.) male, is captive-bred and a good defrost feeder. He is rarely handled, only every month or so, especially when the vivarium is soiled or needs a good clean out. He is tame and has progressed to rats now that he is too big to bother with mice. Feed according to size and every week or so. The amount eaten will vary according to size and appetite, Like many species of snake, some will bathe regularly and others never or seldom. Always offer Carpet Pythons a water bowl, preferably a large one, but they may rarely use it.

Carpet Pythons are suited to keepers able to provide spacious accommodation and need to be well supported when handled.

Common Garter Snake
Thamnophis sirtalis sirtalis

Native to the United States from the Atlantic to the Pacific, these snakes are small, slim, and active. Beautifully marked with creamy lines and reddish flanks, they hunt in largely aquatic environments and will catch and eat both fish and amphibians.

must know

Garter Snakes rely greatly on sight for hunting. As a diurnal predator, they can track by both sight and scent, seizing their prey firmly in the mouth. Prey is generally too small and defenseless to require constriction and most foods are swallowed alive, head first.

Creating the right environment

Over 50 types of Garter Snake exist and can all be kept under similar conditions. An adult pair prefer a 48 x 15 x 15-inch (120 x 38 x 38-cm.) vivarium or larger. Juveniles should be reared in smaller containers. You need a dry vivarium equipped with a good-size water bowl and substrates, such as wood chips, and leaf litter. Logs, branches, and even living ferns may be incorporated, offering spaces to explore and hiding places. A humidity chamber is essential for good skin conditioning. Keep the substrate warm with a heater pad, with a temperature range of 68–79°F (20–26°C). If using spot lamps for overhead heating, they should be controlled by a thermostat.

Handling

These snakes generally handle well—nervous individuals may defecate on you but this is rare and usually only happens while a juvenile or wild-caught snake is going through the first steps of taming.

Feeding

Large water bowls are preferred, and many keepers remove their snakes to another container at feeding time. They should be fed separately if several snakes live together, because they have a tendency to fight over food. When two snakes get hold of the same item, one may eat the other snake as well as the prey. Garters enjoy exercising in a shallow bath, and if fed outside their main vivarium are likely to feed, then defecate, considerably easing your cleaning routine. After defrosting fish for its feed, it may be that simply placing it in a shallow water dish is sufficient to get your snake interested. Initially, it is often best to wriggle the food about a bit on long tweezers. Once the snake recognizes this as "live" food, it will soon learn to accept the same type of food in future from a bowl. Many Garter Snakes will also take small rodents, pinkies, and earthworms.

Breeding

Garter Snakes are live-bearers and the young grow rapidly if fed correctly, maturing at eight to ten months. The number of young can vary between subspecies and depends on the age, experience, and health of the female; between 10 and 80 young per litter is typical. Sperm is retained by females and they may produce young up to two years after one mating.

The keeled scales, each with a ridge, make the enchanting Garter Snake rougher to the touch than many other species.

Rough Green Snake

This gentle, small, grass green, diurnal insect-eating snake is usually found in the vicinity of streams, meadows, and marshes. It is native to the eastern United States from New Jersey to Florida and westward to Texas, Kansas, and into northern Mexico.

must know

All snakes have scales, made from a hard substance called keratin, which is also the basis of hair and feathers. Every species has a different pattern and many have some larger scales called shields. Rough Green snakes have rough or keeled scales, with a ridge in the center. They help give a better grip and can be rubbed together to make a threatening noise.

Creating the right environment

Green Snakes can be kept in groups or on their own, and may share a community vivarium with other similar-size noncannibalistic species, such as Garter Snakes. They enjoy temperatures in the range of 75–82°F (24–28°C), established with the combination of a heater pad and spotlight controlled by a thermostat. They are best housed in a dry but regularly mist-sprayed vivarium; they won't like it too damp but will thrive with slight humidity. You can decorate their vivarium of 36 x 15 x 15 inches (90 x 38 x 38 cm.) with some mosses, a greater depth of leaf litter, and by incorporating a humidity chamber. A lightweight snake, fine branches or house plants will give them something suitable to climb on. Their lifespan is around ten years.

Delicate and beautiful, Green Snakes are a social species that may be kept in groups.

Handling

As their name suggests, these snakes have rough or keeled scales, and they do not slide through the fingers like smooth-scaled snakes. They are, however, simple to handle albeit delicate.

Feeding

One of the things people like most about Rough Green Snakes is that they do not need to be fed rodents but are happy to exist on a diet of insects, such as crickets, spiders, and the occasional small vertebrate. In the wild, they occasionally consume small lizards and frogs, so I advise a varied diet where possible, even offering the occasional nutritious pinkies. They are unlikely to eat dead foods, but are fascinating to watch stalking a big, fat juicy cricket, grasshopper, or millipede. Feed on a regular basis, say, every other day—but avoid mealworms because these are less palatable and less nutritious than crickets and other available live foods.

Breeding

Due to the fact that this is a common snake, little effort has been made to captive breed them on a regular basis, although use of pesticides is severely affecting some populations. They are legally collected and exported under a monitoring system, so do not be concerned about keeping a wild-born snake. Perhaps eventually you will become a Rough Green Snake specialist and breeder. An average of two to six eggs are laid at a time.

Take care when handling Rough Green Snakes because they are delicate.

must know

Rough Green Snakes can reach 36 inches (90 cm.) in length. Semiarboreal, they have superb camouflage, which effectively makes them disappear while climbing low vegetation.

Bull Snake *Pituophis elanoleucus sayi*

Bull Snakes are large and powerful predators that feed almost exclusively on small mammals. Variable in their patterning and coloration, they are one of North America's most attractive snakes.

Habitat and behavior

There are 15 known subspecies, ranging northward just into Canada right down into Central America. Bull Snakes are popular with cereal-growing farmers and are apparently still caught and even purchased for release into barns where they eat rats, mice, and squirrels. They are noted for the noises they make and their violent defense posturing. An irritated or threatened snake inhales a considerable quantity of air, swelling itself to appear larger than it really is. With its open mouth and a typically serpentine "S"- shaped body posture striking up toward its real or imagined foe, it makes a scary encounter. However, like most snakes, even venomous ones, it is largely bluff and the snake would really prefer a hasty retreat than a violent confrontation.

Creating the right environment

A 60 x 24 x 24-inch (150 x 60 x 60-cm.) vivarium is ideal for an adult or breeding pair of these secretive but active snakes. They need a warm and dry vivarium with height because they will climb, but they also enjoy burrowing under the paper or wood chips at ground level. Finer substrates, such as sand, can irritate their skin, so chunkier moss, bark chips, or paper are best. A temperature range of 75–82°F (24–28°C) is adequate, and an under-floor heater pad warming the substrate, is recommended. Use a spot lamp to create a basking area, which must be controlled by a thermostat to avoid overheating.

Water should be available at all time,s although this snake does not enjoy bathing. Occasional mist spraying will help because it is most at home in a semiarid desert or dry-forest type of habitat.

The wide ventral (belly) scales are visible underneath this Bull Snake. They give snakes a good grip on a variety of surfaces and aid movement.

Handling

Juvenile captive-bred specimens are best because they are already adapted to handling. As they grow, the power and potential size of these snakes is apparent. Although they can reach over 7 feet (2.1 m.), 5 feet (1.5 m.) is average, but they are a handful at only 24 inches (60 cm). They are safe to handle but strong and persistent, and are not suitable for unsupervised handling by a child.

Feeding

Bull Snakes are unlikely to refuse any suitably sized mammalian or bird prey; all rodents are accepted. In the wild, their prey may be dug out of their burrows with a combination of the body loops helping to shift soil and an unusual raised scale situated on the tip of the snout. Feed every seven days on average.

Beautifully patterned Bull Snakes are somewhat secretive, but they feed well and are now a popular choice for the herpetologist.

Brazilian Rainbow Boa
Epicrates cenchria cenchria

Rainbow Boas are common in many regions of South America, including Brazil, Guyana, and much of the vast Amazon basin. This naturally nocturnal species inhabits a wide range of conditions, from rain forest to grassy plains and scrubland.

must know

The underlying color of these snakes is a reddish brown hue with rings and spots along the entire length of the body. A variable species for shades of color, the spots and rings tend to fade as the snakes mature to an average of 60 inches (120 cm.) long, but potentially growing to 76 inches (190 cm.).

Iridescent scales

Their name is derived from their iridescent scales, which, like oil on water, display a vivid spectrum of shimmering colors that change according to the light and angle of vision. Rainbow Boa scales have microscopic ridges that act like a prism—refracting sunlight into a stunning show of colors. It probably aids in defense and makes it hard for a predator to pinpoint the exact location of the snake.

Creating the right environment

These snakes are simple to keep and easily tamed. They need a warm, dry vivarium with a temperature range of 72–86°F (22–30°C) with some humidity, but never damp. A 36 x 15 x 15-inch (90 x 38 x 38-cm.) vivarium should be fine for most snakes, or a 48 x 15 x 15-inch (120 x 38 x 38-cm.) one for a larger specimen. An occasional mist spray is sufficient to keep the atmosphere fresh.

Feeding

These are lazy snakes, preferring to wait and ambush their meals instead of giving chase. Like all boas, they are naturally inclined to feed on birds and mammals, the dexterous long jaws opening to consume surprisingly large prey items. The heat-sensitive pits, situated on the mouth, give the snake's brain a thermal image of its warm-blooded prey; thus, it may help if you warm up the food you offer to your snake, so it has a better image of its meal.

Most are kept, grown, and even bred on an exclusively rodent diet. Be careful not to overfeed—avoid obesity in all pets. You should soon notice when a good feeder simply becomes an overeater.

Breeding

Like all boas, these snakes give birth to living young and are a relatively easy species to attempt breeding from, should your interest for them grow. A short cooling-off, or brumation, period is advised before attempting to pair adults. If successful, mating behavior should be seen almost immediately. They can be kept communally but are usually and satisfactorily housed in separate vivariums.

With shimmering body scales, these South American reptiles are a highly desirable pet snake.

Boa Constrictor *Boa constrictor*

Boas are the largest snakes that are most frequently kept and bred in captivity. For decades, they have been a popular pet in the Americas. Their geographic range begins in Mexico and extends southward through Central America down into South America.

must know

Despite their media image—attacking jungle explorers and engulfing or even poisoning large beasts—Boa Constrictors are nonvenomous and placid, nocturnal creatures, preferring to remain hidden during the daytime in hollow logs and old mammal burrows or camouflaged among leaf litter.

Appearance

Boas seem to improve in coloration as you travel south through their range. Among the most desirable of Boa Constrictors are those with red tails—the Red-tailed Boas (*Boa constrictor ortonii*) are native to Peru and are attractive with deep blood red colors along the lower back and tail.

Boas are beautiful snakes with an unusual texture to the touch, which is more fabriclike than scaly. They have a basic creamy, silver coloration with diamond-shaped patterns and a peppering of spots. The coloration of Boas is variable among the 11 recognized, closely related subspecies, but they are all normally very attractive.

Boa Constrictors are 6 feet 8 inches–13 feet 4 inches (2–4 m.) long, but 10-foot (3 m.) specimens are a more common adult size. They are good climbers, feeding on mammals and birds in the wild.

Creating the right environment

Ensure that you really are capable of caring for and housing any snake before you purchase one of these. As a Boa Constrictor grows, it will require larger food items and eventually a big vivarium. A spacious, dry vivarium needs to be warmed within a 77–88°F (25–32°C) range to provide comfort for a

Boa Constrictor. Only sturdy climbing shelves or branches are suitable for such a chunky snake. Cork logs are ideal for offering a sense of security, but Boas are happy to be in full view most of the time. Zoological gardens have long preferred them for show as, unlike many snakes, they may be on display for long periods. Any substrate will suit this species, but avoid sand and the finer grades of wood or bark chips. A large water bowl is welcomed and your Boa will bathe occasionally, often for many hours or days at a time. Mist spray occasionally to freshen up the environment.

Handling

Boa Constrictors are large snakes and should be handled with care. With long teeth and a powerful bite, Boas are best kept and handled under adult

Cryptic coloration helps the Boa Constrictor blend in effectively with its natural environment.

must know

The jaws of snakes are very flexible; with their elastically expandable lower jaw, most species can eat surprisingly large food items. Food is swallowed whole, usually head first. Look out for a snake's yawn: Boas and other snakes may open and stretch their mouths wide after feeding to resettle or realign the jaw.

You need plenty of space to successfully house a snake as large as a Boa in captivity.

supervision, although most pet ones, which are well tamed and cared for, will never bite. Larger specimens may need two or more people to help lift them and maintain control. Tame specimens pose few problems, but an aggressive large Boa requires careful and firm handling. A bite would hurt and require medical attention. To transport a snake, all but the smallest are usually placed in a cloth bag, pillowcase or duvet cover, tied securely at the top. Smaller specimens can be transported in their pet homes.

Feeding

Like all the larger snakes, Boas are best fed with caution. Prey should be dropped onto the floor or wiggled on long tweezers for younger specimens that have not yet adjusted to taking static instead of living food. Boas will accept mice, rats, or small rabbits as well as the occasional chick and young chicken. With a large, greatly expanding jaw and neck, they easily consume prey items much larger than you might imagine possible—until, that is, you get to know snakes better.

Smaller prey

Smaller prey offered in greater quantities may be more efficient if you want to handle your snake regularly, because the smaller items are more quickly digested, making handling less uncomfortable for the Boa. One of the main benefits of having a defrost feeding regime is that snakes are tamer and less likely to be alert to any movement representing a possible food source. They become conditioned to expecting dead static items to eat and are less likely to bite or strike out.

Boa Constrictors have an unusual mottled belly, or ventral scales.

Breeding

Boa Constrictors are relatively easy to breed and they can be seen copulating many times over a few weeks if they are successfully paired. The young develop inside the mother, who will bask more often to keep her developing babies warm. The 30–60 live young, measuring around 19 inches (48 cm.) or so, will feed after their first skin shed and are completely independent from birth.

Waiting for food this Boa is barely visible on the forest floor.

want to know more?

• For numerous articles, photographs, and other web sites, visit: www.kingsnake.com
• Do some research to find a herpetological society local to you. Look on the Internet or ask in local pet stores
• Books are available on the natural history or care of snakes. One of my favorites is *Living Snakes of the World* by John M. Mehrtens (Sterling 1987). Check out your local library, book store, pet store, or the Internet.

5 Invertebrates

Some invertebrates are very attractive and
can make fascinating pets. In fact, they are
the most diverse creatures on our planet,
and we share our world with literally millions
of species, which number many billions of
individuals. Several types are ideal for children
to manage alone, requiring a minimal amount
of cleaning or specialty equipment to maintain.
They frequently have a short natural lifespan
and will never require veterinarian treatments
or grooming. A vivarium can house many
invertebrates, which, with their interesting
life cycles and behavior, make surprisingly
absorbing and educational pets.

What are invertebrates?

The majority of living creatures on earth are invertebrates, and a single swarm of locusts can contain more individuals than the whole human population. Invertebrates include all the animals without backbones, such as the squid and clam, as well as the familiar creepy crawlies, such as insects, worms, and spiders.

must know

Many invertebrates have a special body structure called an exoskeleton, which is a hard external shell, as seen on a millipede or Praying Mantis. Other species, such as worms, are composed entirely of soft tissues.

Ectotherms

All invertebrates are ectotherms, which means they are reliant on external sources of heat to maintain their bodily functions. Interestingly, some species have been found to survive in extreme conditions, both above and below what scientists conventionally term fatal temperatures—for example, under ice caps and at volcanic thermal vents.

Feeding and diet

Invertebrates consume a variety of foods; some, such as Praying Mantids and spiders, are carnivores, while others, such as Stick Insects and Leaf Insects, are herbivores. Cockroaches, however, are scavengers, willing to consume almost anything available. Depending on the species, foods may be grazed, hunted, ambushed, trapped, snared, or even lured.

Handling

In general, inverts are the least handleable of all the animals featured in this book. If in doubt, don't handle them. They should not be moved or handled during a molt, when they are very vulnerable to damage. Soon after a molt, an invertebrate's body hardens and they can then be handled if necessary.

Adult supervision is essential when young pet keepers want to move or handle these creatures. Only a few species are suitable to keep as household pets.

Arthropods

All the invertebrates in this book are classified as Arthropods—animals with an external skeleton and jointed limbs. Arthropods have to regularly shed their external skeleton or exoskeleton as they grow. Most belong to several major groups, as listed below.

Insects

All have three pairs of legs and three parts to the body: the head, thorax, and abdomen. Stick Insects, Leaf Insects, and Praying Mantids are all insects.

Millipedes

Millipedes have many body segments and elongated bodies. Each body segment has two pairs of legs. Their close relative, the Centipede, has a single pair of legs per body segment and is a venomous predator, whereas Millipedes are herbivores.

Crustaceans

Crustaceans are characterized as being mainly aquatic hard-shelled creatures, but the Hermit Crab is land based although it still breathes through gills.

Arachnids

Spiders and Scorpions, along with Harvestmen, ticks, and mites, are types of arachnids. They have eight jointed legs and, frequently, two main body parts: the cephalothorax and abdomen.

must know

Invertebrates have essential roles in most ecosystems. They not only eat and recycle rotting vegetation but they inhabit the inside and outside of most other living creatures. They may be found living on all continents, from high peaks to deep underground and in both fresh and saltwater environments.

Invertebrates are found in seemingly endless variety. While many lack legs, wings, and even an exoskeleton, this Praying Mantis is a classic insect.

Indian Stick Insect *Carausius morosus*

Indian Stick Insects are one of the easiest of all the invertebrates to manage, and, they are a good introduction to keeping and learning about insects. Their bodies are long and sticklike, growing to 4 inches (11 cm.), and they live for a year.

must know

Care must be taken if keeping cut plants in jars of water because the Stick Insects can fall in and drown. Try to find narrow-necked jars or pierce holes in the lids of water-filled containers.

Appearance and behavior

Stick Insects are usually green or brown with bright red markings on the inside of their forelegs, which are flashed as a warning when they are disturbed. If threatened, they often drop to the ground and remain motionless like a twig. When the threat has passed, they stretch out their legs and start moving again, gently swaying like a twig in the breeze.

Creating the right environment

These insects require a tall vivarium measuring at least 12 x 18 x 12 inches (30 x 45 x 30 cm.), because they live mainly on food plants. Keep them warm at around 75°F (24°C). However, they are a tolerant species and are happy at room temperature, although they dislike temperature extremes.

Humidity levels

A reasonable level of humidity is required, so mist spray but do not let them get soggy or moldy. A thirsty Stick Insect exercises its mouth parts continuously and a quick spray of droplets onto a leaf soon quenches its thirst. Paper is good for lining the floor of the vivarium because it is easy to remove for cleaning, but damp leaves or moss may look nicer and increase humidity levels.

Each tiny egg is like a small jar. The baby Stick Insect must pry open the lid to emerge.

Handling

These creatures tame easily but need careful handling. Gently pick up your insect between finger and thumb, or offer your flat palm and tap the creature gently so that it walks onto your hand. Legs that get stuck or hooked onto an object or piece of clothing need a gentle nudge to loosen their grip.

Feeding

Herbivorous by nature, Stick Insects eat only plant matter throughout their entire lives. Most are reared on privet or blackberry leaves and will prefer tender new leaves on young plants. These should be potted and changed regularly to ensure an abundant supply. Freshly cut sprigs of privet or leafy lengths of blackberry can be used, but unpotted stems need replacing frequently.

Breeding

Stick Insects are capable of reproducing without mating. An adult female lays fertilized eggs, measuring $1/8$ inch (2–3 mm.). Hundreds of tiny eggs are laid during her lifetime, several a day during the peak of fertility. Hatch the eggs on vermiculite or sand, keeping them warm and spraying occasionally. Check them periodically. They can take up to a year to hatch. The young require the same conditions as adults but keep them with similar-size individuals. They will molt (shed their skin) six times before reaching adulthood, only a few months later.

Indian Stick Insects not only live on but also eat plants, such as privet, a commonly available and fast-growing plant.

Leaf Insect *Phyllium sp.*

These incredible little creatures look just like the leaves they feed on. Green and flat, they even develop brown spots and rough edges to affect superb camouflage. They are native to warm, humid rain forests in Asia—Malaysia and Thailand—as well as New Guinea, Australia, Madagascar, and the Seychelles.

must know

Depending on the species, the adults measure 3–6 inches (8–15 cm.) long. Leaf Insects are shorter lived and more difficult to maintain and breed than Stick Insects, but are well worth the effort.

This juvenile Leaf Insect, seen alongside a pencil for scale, is one of the many remarkable insects that may be kept in a large group.

Creating the right environment

A 24 x 18 x 12-inch (60 x 45 x 30-cm.) vivarium will house up to six individuals. They prefer temperatures of 70–80°F (21–27°C) but do not like stagnant air. Good ventilation is essential for optimum growth and development, especially during a molt. Maintain the temperature with heater pads or keep in the warmest part of the house.

Because Leaf Insects are arboreal, choice of substrate is largely decorative. Plain paper should be placed on the base of the vivarium when they are breeding, so the eggs can be located easily. Wood chips or even moss, kept moist, help to keep humidity at about 70 percent. Regular mist spraying with tepid water and a hygrometer are recommended, but after a while you will get to know when they are satisfied with your efforts to create a home for them.

Handling

Adults can be encouraged to walk onto your hand. They wobble about in a comical fashion, trying to convince you that they are a leaf blowing in the breeze. Handle them with care because it is so easy to damage these very delicate creatures.

Feeding

In captivity, Leaf Insects live and feed on blackberry leaves. Old cut sprigs need replacing every other day, or, ideally, small plants can be potted and placed directly in the vivarium, then rotated to ensure that fresh growths are available. You can also try them on oak, guava, and rambutan leaves.

Breeding

These small invertebrates have a life expectancy measured in months, not years, and at about four months of age they are ready to breed. Males have slimmer bodies, longer wings, and antennae. One hundred or more eggs are produced and drop to the ground. These, amazingly, are also camouflaged and look like the droppings of caterpillars. The parents die not long after they have finished laying eggs. By keeping the eggs warm, the young will emerge anytime from a few months to over a year later. Tiny bright red (antlike) babies will climb onto plants and start feeding immediately. If you are successful with these insects, you can maintain a constant life cycle with eggs, growing babies, and adults laying at the same time.

A spectacular natural mimic relying entirely on camouflage for its defense, the Leaf Insect is unable to defend itself in any way except its leaflike disguise.

Giant Millipede *Epibolus sp.*

In Africa, these creatures are called "chongaloloo" or "jungle trains." Of the 10,000 types of millipede known, only a few are regularly kept as pets, and among them is the Giant Millipede, which is essentially an animal of the soil and leaf litter.

must know

To check the humidity in your pets' container, squeeze a leaf in your hand. It should curl, neither cracking (too dry) nor seeping any water (too wet).

Appearance and behavior

Giant Millipedes are easy to establish and breed if several are kept together as a colony. They may be reddish brown or black, and some species are even striped. Growing to 10 inches (25 cm.), they can live for several years if kept in the right conditions. Millipedes are slow, harmless terrestrial scavengers and should not be confused with centipedes.

Creating the right environment

You need a large and wide, instead of high, container. One measuring 36 x 18 x 12 inches (90 x 45 x 30 cm.) or 24 x 12 x 12 inches (60 x 30 x 30 cm.) is a suitable home. Add chemical/fertilizer-free compost to a depth of 3–4 inches (8–10 cm.) and cover with leaf litter. Maintain a temperature of 75–80°F (24–27°C) using heater pads. Keep the vivarium humid and balanced somewhere between dry and damp. A setup like this will only need cleaning out completely once or twice a year.

Feeding

Oak, sycamore, and vine leaves, among others, and various mosses are ideal. I advise prefreezing leaves in bags in order to avoid introducing other invertebrates into your setup. Besides eating leaf

This tamed Millipede is crawling on its keeper's hand. If disturbed, it would rapidly curl up into a defensive coil.

litter, small pieces of fruit and vegetables can also be offered on shallow dishes or upturned lids, so they are easy to remove before spoiling. Leaf litter should be added liberally to a depth of several inches and added to as it gets consumed. Millipedes will drink from mist sprayed droplets or very shallow container lids or dishes.

Handling

If you are gentle, Millipedes tame quickly, and it's an amazing feeling to have one on your hand. Their legs move in ripples like a Mexican wave. They are active at night or under crepuscular (low-light) conditions. Many species can secrete unpleasant fluids from glands along the sides of the body when disturbed or irritated—these may smell, sting, or stain hands and clothing. They also curl when disturbed, while sleeping, or during a molt, when they remain inactive for a while and should not be disturbed.

Each body segment is supported by two pairs of legs, and every leg has tiny hooks, which enable the Millipede to travel quickly along the ground.

Breeding

Males are easily sexed if viewed from underneath—gonopods are visible on the seventh or eighth segment. These are modified legs for transferring sperm to the females. In males, they are frequently hidden from view—you may just see a stump. Millipedes wrap around each other to mate, and some then build a nest in which to lay eggs. Should yours breed, you would soon notice numerous babies crawling around the leaf litter. Initially, these have far fewer segments and legs than adults, but as they shed and grow, these soon develop.

These tiny 2-inch (6-cm.) captive-bred juvenile Millipedes are ready to move to a new home and start their own colony.

Praying Mantis *Sphodromantis sp*

The awesome Praying Mantis is a familiar creature to many people who live in the warmer parts of the world. At least one European type, *Mantis religiosa*, was introduced into the United States early in the last century, and it is now widespread and considered a naturalized species.

Mantids are best held by letting them crawl up and onto your hand. They will not tolerate being held between thumb and finger.

Appearance and behavior

Many varieties are available for the pet keeper, and they are usually green or brown in color, reaching 3 inches (7-8 cm.) in length. One particularly attractive species is the Orchid Mantis (*Hymenopus coronatus*), which is a shade of pink and closely resembles the flower blooms it rests upon while awaiting visiting insects. The Praying Mantis is a voracious predator. It can actively stalk its prey or can wait patiently camouflaged against foliage for an insect to venture within striking range. Upon close examination, we can see that Mantids are well designed for killing. The long front legs are lined with numerous spines and a curved hook, which, in a fraction of a second, snatches and impales the unsuspecting insect. Once held, the prey's fate is sealed and the Mantis starts to consume it.

Creating the right environment

Praying Mantids are generally purchased as nymphs, individually packed in small plastic containers. Measuring less than an inch in length, the Mantis needs a twig to climb upon and fruit flies or other mini bugs to feed on. As the Mantis feeds and needs to grow, it will molt, reaching its next development stage, which is known as an instar. After it has molted several times, larger accommodation should be offered. A vivarium that is 12 x 18 x 12 inches (30 x 45 x 30 cm) is ideal, and it can be heated, if required, by a spot lamp or heater pad. These creatures like to be kept at a temperature of around 75°F (24°C)—this can drop a few degrees at night with no ill effects.

As arboreal invertebrates, Mantids need to be provided with something to climb upon. Branches, twigs, foliage, and other decorations are all suitable and make an attractive home for you and your Mantis to enjoy. A living plant helps to enhance any display. A fluorescent lamp will assist in plant growth as well as light the vivarium to effectively. Mantids are cannibalistic and should be kept individually.

The only insect that can turn its head and look over its shoulder at you, Praying Mantids are a simple to keep pet.

A voracious predator, this Praying Mantis has caught and is consuming a cricket.

Handling

For closer examination, you can encourage a Mantis onto the palm of your hand, where it will move around happily. Don't attempt to pick one up using a finger or thumb because the Mantis will jab you with its forearms. Be warned that adult Mantids can fly, so ensure that all the doors and windows are closed just in case.

Feeding

Mantids will eat almost any live foods they can catch and hold. The very smallest need fruit flies, micro crickets, or aphids, but once they begin to grow they will quickly graduate to larger prey, such as crickets, butterflies, and houseflies. In the wild, even bees and wasps will be eaten. Feed them as much as they will eat, but do not leave too much live food in the vivarium because they can distress the Mantis if it feels overrun. They are messy feeders, leaving discarded legs, wings, and other body parts around the vivarium. Remove them regularly, along with any mantis faecal pellets.

Breeding

Mantids are essentially an annual species, with offspring emerging each spring. If lucky, they survive to mature, mate, and, if female, lay eggs before dying within the same year. Your pet Mantis is, therefore, relatively short lived, taking six months to mature and then living for approximately six months as an adult. By growing several nymphs to maturity, you have a good chance of breeding them. Females are easily distinguished from males. They have six visible segments on the underside of their abdomen, whereas males have eight. Mating is a dangerous time for males—they may be eaten while attempting to mate, during mating, or immediately afterward. One female may produce several egg cases (oothecae) from a successful mating. Even unmated females will lay eggs, but these won't hatch.

The new generation emerge in great numbers from each egg case, which may hold 20-200 eggs. Newly emerged Mantids are the size of a mosquito and are miniature versions of the adults. Like all insects, by the time they have reached adulthood they have wings and can fly. The appearance of wings establishes that maturity has been reached and the Mantids are ready to breed.

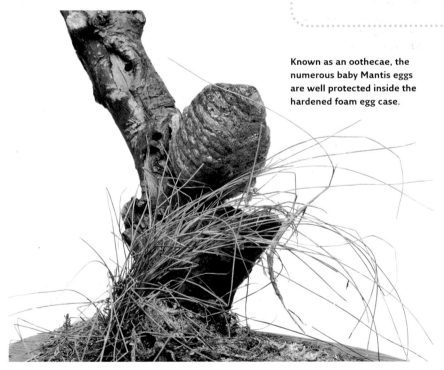

Known as an oothecae, the numerous baby Mantis eggs are well protected inside the hardened foam egg case.

Hermit Crab *Ceonobita sp.*

Land Hermit Crabs are found in the warmer parts of the world, including North America, Australia, and Asia. They are well adapted for life on land, burrowing into sand or under tree roots in humid habitats. Up to 13 species are known, and, depending on where you live, several make interesting pets.

must know

Hermit Crabs return to the sea to breed, with the eggs hatching into tiny free-swimming larvae that eventually return to dry land as tiny crabs, so they will not breed in captivity. Fortunately, most species are common and live longer as pets than in the wild.

Appearance and behavior

Hermit Crabs are available in a variety of colors, ranging from pink or reddish brown to sandy yellow. They use the empty shells of other marine or land snails as a home and for protection, changing these regularly as they molt and grow. They vary in size considerably, from 2 inches (5 cm.) up to 6 inches (15 cm.), and live for over ten years.

Creating the right environment

Hermit Crabs are, in fact, very social animals and should be kept in groups. They are active mostly at night. A substrate of either fine beach sand or coral and reef sands is fine, but some people keep them successfully on river pebbles and/or coconut fiber. The important thing is that they need to burrow, especially when a molt is due. The larger the aquarium/vivarium you can provide, the better for offering a range of substrates at varying depths. They need to be heated to between 72–80°F (22–27°C), if you do not have a warm enough house, by heater pads or a lamp—follow the instructions carefully. Humidity of 70–80 percent, without allowing the air to stagnate, is important.

An absolute necessity is plenty of options for

changing shells. Any pet store that sells these crabs should have a selection of sizes and types to tempt your growing pet into selecting some more suitable accommodation. Some will change shells every few weeks given the opportunity. Children are particularly drawn to the highly colorful painted shells at pet stores, but a variety of options is more important to the crab than color.

Initially nervous of handling, this Hermit Crab has retreated into its shell for protection.

Handling

These crabs are generally nonaggressive but can pinch with their claws. Simply lift them by the shell and place on your hand. As they get accustomed to you, they will amble about happily from hand to hand, retreating into the shell when nervous. Make sure you are seated to ensure that you do not drop them, especially if they pinch you with their claws. Never try to pull one from its shell.

Much enjoyment can be gained from watching these comical creatures shuffle around the vivarium looking for food and new accommodation.

Feeding

These are omnivorous scavengers, so almost anything goes foodwise. Pet stores frequently sell Hermit Crab foods, and these are usually good enough, but they will also eat small pieces of carrot, banana, coconut, fish flakes and pellets, salad greens, and even bits of meat. Avoid citrus fruit and anything spicy or processed. They will benefit from natural unbleached beach debris, such as cuttlefish, driftwood, and natural corals and sponges, which will be nibbled at. A shallow bowl of fresh water and another of salty seawater are recommended, along with a shallow food bowl that is changed before spoiling.

Molting

At regular intervals, Hermit Crabs need to molt. This is the most difficult part of their care to get right. Generally, they become sluggish before a molt and may even appear dead if you are not used to this change. They either hide under a root or burrow into a sandy mixture in a damper part of their home. They are most vulnerable at this time and are best removed from a colony to a separate molting tank until the process is completed. At this stage, some new shell options will be appreciated and they will be eager to feed. They must be kept humid.

Unlike these plain old sea shells, glossy painted shells that are suitable for Hermit Crabs can be bought at many pet stores.

Curly-Haired Tarantula
Brachypelma albopilosa

There are around 800 species of Tarantula. These large, hairy spiders often have appealing colors and markings and make a popular low-cost pet, requiring only the minimum of time and space to maintain them in excellent condition.

Popular pets
It is best to buy one as a spiderling—they are bred in large numbers in Europe and North America to satisfy demand. The most popular and passive are those from North, Central, and South America. One of these, the Curly-Haired Tarantula, is a favorite of mine, and I have a specimen of around 30 years of age that has been handled for many years without ever once causing me any concerns.

Creating the right environment
Most Tarantulas not only thrive in but also seem to prefer small vivariums, and although some species may live communally, the Curly-Haired and other terrestrial species featured in this book should be housed alone. A 12 x 12 x 12-inch (30 x 30 x 30-cm.) vivarium is fine, although a larger unit does give you more scope to create an attractive naturalistic display. They need a retreat and some wood chips or vermiculite mixed together to make a good substrate. Maintain at 75-84°F (24-29°C).

Handling
Not everyone wants to handle their pet Tarantula and that is fine, but should you want to, then it is

must know

No record can be found of human deaths caused by a Tarantula bite— they are not a species considered dangerous to man. They are usually portrayed as aggressive and deadly, but while they are predators and do have large fangs, most are mild mannered and are unlikely to even try to bite their carer.

Despite their fearsome reputation, many Tarantulas make attractive if somewhat unusual pets.

important to never drop your pet. Although these spiders are robust animals, the legs and abdomen can be injured easily in a fall. They should not be allowed to climb onto clothing, because the tiny hooks in their legs get stuck in fabric. Tarantulas can bite, but it is a rare event. However, the abdominal hairs can cause an allergic reaction, so be careful not to touch them here—just stroke the legs.

Feeding

Most pet spiders like mine live on a diet of crickets. Variety is good, however, and occasionally I will offer something different, such as a nontoxic caterpillar, beetle grub, or locust hopper. In the wild, they would attempt to eat almost any small vertebrate or invertebrate they can overpower.

Breeding

Breeding Tarantulas provides a fascinating insight into the precarious mating habits of spiders. You are, if successful, likely to feel euphoric at your achievement in helping to bring new lives into the world (400–600 of them). Considerable time and effort will be required to ensure their initial survival and subsequent development. A male that is ready to mate will deposit some sperm onto a small sheet of web. He will then dip his pedipalp into the sperm and proceed to visit any potential mates. The females release an attractant scent that draws him into a potentially fatal meeting. If the male finds a willing partner, he will hold her fangs with his mating hooks and insert and empty his sperm into her genital opening. So far so good—then he will beat a hasty retreat, but frequently the female will turn on him and eat him.

Molting spiders

When a Tarantula is found upside down with curled-up legs, it is probably just molting. Do not disturb it but remove any uneaten live foods still present in the vivarium. It can take between one and two days for an adult to complete the process. Spiderlings molt very regularly because they grow quickly. Adults do so less frequently, molting on average once a year. Soon after molting or shedding, Tarantulas are normally eager to drink and feed, but it takes another day or so for their new exoskeleton to harden completely.

Always handle your pet with care. Many Tarantula owners regularly handle their spiders but ensure that they do so with caution.

Mexican Red Kneed Tarantula
Brachypelma smithi

These are one of the most striking Tarantulas—large with a leg span of 6–7 inches (15–18 cm.). The body is dark brown with bright red on all leg joints and pedipalps, making them a popular pet. Females can live for 30 years, but a male's life span is limited.

must know

This spider is a protected and threatened species, with its natural habitat along the central Pacific coast in Mexico under continuing pressure from land clearing for ranching, agriculture, and housing. However, fortunately for the pet keeper, they are widely bred in captivity.

Creating the right environment

These spiders inhabit dry, scrubby desert but like humidity levels of around 70 percent. A shallow water dish helps provide this, as well as drinking water. A mix of vermiculite and wood chips about $3^1/_2$ inches (9 cm.) deep will provide ample opportunity to dig a burrow.

A piece of cork bark or half a flowerpot on its side can be used as a retreat. A minimum vivarium size of 12 x 12 x 12 inches (30 x 30 x 30 cm.) is adequate, warmed from below by a heater pad covering no more than half the area and controlled by a thermostat to 75–82°F (24–28°C).

Alternatively, a lamp over part of the unit may be used to warm the spiders.

Handling

Handling should be initiated at an early age, so the spider and handler gradually get used to each other. The spider should be gently nudged on the legs to encourage it to walk onto your hands. Occasionally skittish, be especially careful to avoid touching the urticating (stinging/itchy) hairs of the abdomen that may be rubbed off in a cloud when the spider is irritated. Always wash your hands after touching Tarantulas and remember that many people keep them but never try or want to handle them.

Feeding

This spider is a nocturnal hunter with the tips of all its legs sensitive to smells, tastes, and vibration. It will tackle a variety of prey from insects to frogs, lizards, and rodents.

The prey is held and venom is injected from both fangs to paralyze it and begin digestion before the body is sucked dry, leaving a hollow skin or exoskeleton behind. In captivity, crickets are the established offering, but locusts and other prey can be offered for variety.

must know

To breed these spiders, see page 181. Mexican Red Kneed and other Tarantula males can, upon maturing, molt, and they are readily identified by the two mating hooks on the underside of the front pair of legs.

This species is traditionally used for human contact at many zoos and wildlife parks. However, some individuals are easily irritated and would not be suitable for handling.

Chilean Rose Tarantula *Grammostola rosea*

These are attractive, fluffy-looking spiders with a salmon pink or rosy red hue. They are often seen on breeders' lists or in pet stores at 1 inch (2–3 cm.) in size—the ideal time to acquire one. They occur in South America in Chile, Argentina, and Bolivia.

must know

Confusingly for the hobbyist, this species has undergone several taxonomic (science of classification) name changes, and you may see them in books or on web sites as *Grammostola cala* or *spatulata* and *rosea*. However, they are always commonly referred to as Chilean Rose Tarantulas.

Creating the right environment

Chilean Rose Tarantulas should always be kept alone; like most spiders, they are not social animals. They are content and safe on their own and do not feel lonely. This species is less likely to use burrows than many other Tarantula types but must still be offered a retreat or two to hide in. I have kept them in the larger plastic pet homes but a 12 x 12 x 12-inch (30 x 30 x 30-cm.) vivarium is just fine. They need to be kept warm at around 79–82°F (26–28°C) but not as warm as some species—a warm room is likely to be sufficient. If you can give one a larger vivarium

It is amazing to see how arthropods change their exoskeleton to grow and you have a good chance of observing this with spiders.

of, say, 24 x 12 x 12 inches (60 x 30 x 30 cm.) with multiple retreats and heat the warm part of the unit with a lamp or heater pad, but, judging by where they prefer to live, you will get a good understanding of their preferences. A 2-inch (5-6-cm.) depth of vermiculite mix is good as a base, and a couple of retreats should be provided along with a shallow water dish. Probably once, maybe twice, a year a clean out is required. Move your spider to a small escape-proof tub while you thoroughly clean the entire unit, replacing the old substrate.

Tarantulas can be handled on a regular basis without incident. Their dangerous image belies their usually gentle nature.

Handling

This is another popular handling species, but adult attention should always be given when children are attempting to pick up a spider, and be careful to avoid the irritating hairs of the abdomen.

Feeding

Most captive-reared Tarantulas live pretty much on crickets, locusts, or hoppers. As with all live foods, it is important that they have been well fed and cared for to ensure their nutritious content. A few bugs can be left with the spider, so it can hunt at will, apart from when a molt is due. If the spider seems irritated by excess live food, remove it at once.

Breeding

Female Chilean Rose Tarantulas probably live for around 15 years in captivity, while males reach a final maturing molt at around two years of age. Their days are then numbered.

Imperial Scorpion *Pandinus imperator*

These scorpions are the world's largest, up to 8 inches (20 cm.), but they are easy to care for and not dangerous. Native to Central and West African forests, they hide beneath rotten logs and leaf litter.

must know

With savage pincers and a poison gland in her tail, an amorous male approaches a female with great caution. He grabs her pincers, and, with her weapons safely controlled, they dance, shuffling forward and backward. The male deposits a pack of sperm on the ground and, as he pulls her over it, the female takes up the tiny package into her body. To avoid becoming her supper, the male quickly releases his hold and they separate.

Creating the right environment

Spending time hidden or hunting in leaf litter, the Imperial Scorpion likes a good ground covering. A depth of up to 6 inches (15 cm.) of vermiculite and leaf litter will replicate its forest habitat. A retreat is essential to make it feel secure. A small colony of four to ten scorpions may be housed together for breeding purposes, as long as ample retreats and food are available. A 48 x 12 x 12-inch (120 x 30 x 30-cm.) vivarium is adequate. Some fighting is inevitable within a colony, and occasionally a specimen may be devoured by its friends. For this reason, many people prefer to keep them separately. Heating by pad is recommended—they need ground warmth, to 77–86°F (25–30°C). Mist spray regularly to maintain humidity levels, and provide a shallow water dish.

Handling

Most people keep these scorpions for their aesthetic pleasure and enjoy watching their behavior. I don't recommend that novices or young people handle scorpions. However, some people do enjoy picking them up by quickly and firmly holding the scorpion by its bulbous sting and placing it in the palm of the hand. However, be warned as temperaments vary. They can pinch hard with their claws and a sting will hurt, but generally this species is passive.

Feeding

As predatory arachnids, these creatures prefer slow-moving prey, such as large grubs and caterpillars. Dead mice, pinkies, locusts, and crickets are all taken. Offer food twice weekly by releasing insects into the vivarium or by offering food, using long tweezers, directly to the scorpion's pincers.

Breeding

After mating (see opposite), eventually 20–50 live young appear as small white spots crawling on the mother's back. Once the young have molted and darkened, they leave the mother to fend for themselves. At this stage, they should be separated from the parent's vivarium. Maturing Imperial Scorpions shed their exoskeleton about once a year.

These giant African Scorpions, unlike many of their relatives, are not considered dangerous.

want to know more?

• Information about invertebrates can be found in most local libraries and book stores as well as on the Internet. Look at the following web sites:
www.si.edu
www.bugwise.net.au
www.whatsthatbug.com

Need to know more?

Clubs, societies and web sites

There are numerous organizations and web sites that are dedicated to the care of reptiles, amphibians, and invertebrates. They are also a good source of up-to-date information on events and shows. Using the Internet, you can find information that is relevant to you and where you live. Listed below are some useful resources. They often have useful links.

The American Arachnological Society
Founded to promote the study of arachnids.
www.americanarachnology.org/

The American Tarantula Society
A nonprofit organization dedicated to furthering education about tarantulas and other arachnids.
www.atshq.org/

American Tortoise Rescue
Provides links to societies and groups throughout the country and advice on caring for these pets.
www.atshq.org/

The Center for North American Herpetology
Promotes the preservation and conservation of North American amphibians and reptiles.
www.cnah.org/

The Greater Cincinnati Herpetological Society
An organization that is committed to increasing the understanding of reptiles and amphibians, with useful links to other web sites.
www.cincyherp.com

Kingsnake.com
A web portal for all herpetologists, this will help you find Internet links to breeders and dealers as well as general information on reptiles from sites all over the world.
www.kingsnake.com

Society for the Study of Amphibians and Reptiles
Brings conservation issues that affect reptiles and amphibians to the attention of governmental and other agencies and herpetologists throughout worldwide.
www.ssarherps.org

Turtle Homes

Nonprofit organization dedicated to the safety and welfare of turtles and tortoises worldwide.
www.turtlehomes.org

Magazines

There are several magazines dedicated to providing information for the reptile enthusiast.

Reptiles Magazine

A monthly American published magazine also available in Europe with a good website.
www.reptilesmagazine.com

Reptile Hobbyist Magazine

An American publication.
www.tfh.com

Reptilia Magazine

A European bimonthly magazine, published in Spanish, German, English, and Italian editions.
www.reptilia.net

Further reading

Arnold, E. N., and Burton, J. A., *A Field Guide to the Reptiles and Amphibians of Britain and Europe* (HarperCollins, 1996)
Bateman, Rev. Gregory, *The Vivarium* (Upcott Gill, 1897)
Bellairs, A., and Carrington, R., *The World of Reptiles* (Chatto and Windus, 1966)
Berenbaum, May R., *Bugs in the System* (Addison Wesley, 1995)
Fabre, J. H., *The Insect World of J. Henri Fabre* (Beacon Press, Boston, 1991)
Ferguson, G., and de Vosjoli, P. (Eds.), *Care and Breeding Panther, Veiled and Parsons Chameleons* (Advanced Vivarium Systems, USA, 1995)
Mattison, Chris, *Care of Reptiles & Amphibians in Captivity* (Blandford Press, 1983)
Mehrtens, John M., *Living Snakes of the World* (Sterling Publishing Co, 1987)
Necas, Petr, *Chameleons: Nature's Hidden Jewels* (Krieger Publishing, 1999)
Pfeffer, Pierre (Ed.), *Predators and Predation* (Facts on File Inc., New York, 1989)
Smith, Hobart M., *Handbook of Lizards* (Comstock Publishing, 1946)
de Vosjoli, Phillipe, *General Care and Maintenance of Leopard Geckos* (Advanced Vivarium Systems, USA, 1990)
de Vosjoli, Phillipe, *Lizard Keeper's Handbook* (Advanced Vivarium Systems, USA, 1994)

Acknowledgments

Thanks to Jenny, Jack, and Georgia, Simon Murrell, Jed Currey, and all the snakes, lizards, and invertebrates that know me.

Index